TABLE OF CONTENTS

Hannah conceived and gave birth to a son.
She named him Samuel (1:20).

—— 1 ——

Samuel,
a Prophet of the Lord
1 Samuel 1–3

DIMENSION ONE:
WHAT DOES THE BIBLE SAY?

Answer these questions by reading 1 Samuel 1

1. Which of Elkanah's wives has no children? (1:1-2)

2. Where does Elkanah go to sacrifice, and who is the priest there? (1:3-5)

3. Why does Hannah's rival provoke her? (1:6)

4. What vow does Hannah make to the Lord? (1:11)

5. How does Eli react to Hannah's praying in the Temple? (1:12-17)

6. How does God answer Hannah's prayer? (1:19-20)

Answer these questions by reading 1 Samuel 2

7. How does Hannah describe God in her song? (2:1-10)

8. What sins do Hophni and Phinehas, the sons of Eli, commit? (2:17, 22)

9. What is the Lord's attitude toward Samuel? (2:26)

10. As a consequence of the sins of Eli's sons, what will happen to them? (2:34)

Answer these questions by reading 1 Samuel 3

11. Where is Samuel when the Lord first speaks to him? (3:3)

12. Why does Samuel fail to recognize the Lord when God speaks to him? (3:7)

13. How does Eli advise Samuel to respond to God's voice? (3:9)

14. What will God do to the house of Eli? (3:13-14)

15. How does Eli react to Samuel's message from the Lord? (3:17-18)

16. What does Israel know about Samuel? (3:20)

DIMENSION TWO:
WHAT DOES THE BIBLE MEAN?

Background Information on Samuel

In this lesson on 1 Samuel 1–3, there are three main sections: (1) the miraculous and wondrous birth of Samuel; (2) the cultic sins of Hophni and Phinehas, sons of Eli; and (3) Samuel's prophetic call.

Except for minor interruptions, these three chapters flow together around the main theme of Samuel's timely and distinguished servanthood to the Lord. His extraordinary birth, his consecration into the Shiloh priesthood, and his prophetic call from the Lord all clearly confirm Samuel as the principal spokesman for the Lord at this time. His rapid rise into God's favor contrasts sharply with the demise of Eli's two sons.

Through Samuel, God is about to do something truly significant among the chosen people. The coming lessons in this series on 1 and 2 Samuel will disclose exactly what God's actions are. Now, however, let us examine how the Lord prepares and calls Samuel into service.

Samuel is the last in a series of Old Testament figures called *judges*. These persons include Samson, Gideon, Deborah, and many others. These judges serve as temporary military and religious leaders of Israel during the twelfth and eleventh centuries B.C. This period, described in the Old Testament Book of Judges, is a transitional time between the Exodus and the reigns of David and Solomon. These were truly difficult days for Israel, characterized by the Philistine military threat on the one hand, and the religious temptations toward Baal-ism on the other hand. God's guidance of the chosen people during this exciting period is one of the remarkable chapters in the Old Testament. Samuel was a central figure in this crucial time.

1 Samuel 1—The Birth of Samuel

We read at the beginning of this chapter that Elkanah goes annually to Shiloh to offer sacrifices to God. Shiloh (located about twenty miles north of Jerusalem) was an important cultic site in Israel's early history. (See Joshua 18:1; Judges 21:19.) Families made periodic visits to Shiloh to offer sacrifices to the Lord. The Hebrews, along with many other people in the ancient Near East, believed that sacrifices, sacred meals, and pilgrimages were the principal methods of fulfilling their responsibility toward God. These rituals also made amends for personal sin and secured God's continued blessing in their lives.

Elkanah, the father of Samuel, is a very faithful man, by virtue of his annual visits to Shiloh. He is also a very important man, judging from the length of his lineage, dating back to his great grandfather.

Unfortunately, one of his two wives, Hannah, is childless and consequently is the victim of thoughtless abuse from the other wife. In the minds of ancient people, childlessness is a judgment from God. That Samuel comes from a previously childless woman of great faith and piety, as a result of her vow to consecrate him to the Lord's service, clearly shows us that he is destined to greatness. Hannah's promise to leave Samuel's head unshaven is characteristic of the practices of an ancient religious cult known as the Nazirites. They are known for their great piety and utter devotion to God. Samson was also a Nazirite.

Hannah dedicates Samuel to be born to the service of the Lord in the priesthood at Shiloh. Her action indicates Samuel's important role in the history of Israel. The Hebrew expression *I have asked him of the Lord* and the name *Samuel* are similar.

Following a prolonged weaning period, typical in the ancient Near East, Hannah brings the young child to the sanctuary at Shiloh. She presents him to the Lord and to Eli, the old priest. The child who was "asked of the Lord" now becomes the one who is "given over to the Lord" (verse 28). Since sanctuaries such as Shiloh were thought to be earthly abodes of God, it is entirely appropriate that Samuel begin his religious leadership there.

1 Samuel 2:1-10—The Song of Hannah

Although this beautiful thanksgiving hymn praising the Lord's majestic power interrupts the story of Samuel's early life, it nevertheless is an important addition. The hymn celebrates the triumphal power and love of God on behalf of the powerless and the weak. It also provides an important theological understanding of the birth of this child who is shortly to occupy a prominent place among the people of God. Samuel's birth is no mere day-to-day event, nor is Samuel to be yet another judge. Just as his birth is considered a special act of God, so his life under God's supervision will be special in the history of Israel.

1 Samuel 2:12-26—The Sins of Hophni and Phinehas

This section describes the wickedness of Eli's two worthless sons, Hophni and Phinehas. Their behavior strongly contrasts the faithfulness and piety of Samuel. Verses 12-17 describe their sins as cultic in nature, indicating how base they are. They even sin against the Lord. They demand the portions of the sacrificial food usually reserved for the Lord, and they sexually violate the women who serve as Temple aides. Such actions do not go unnoticed by God.

By contrast, Samuel continues his priestly apprenticeship and grows in favor with God. He even wears a little robe clearly marking him as a duly authorized servant of the Lord (verse 19).

Although he is not directly responsible for the sins of his sons, Eli lacks the strength to temper their evil conduct. Their misdeeds worsen with each passing day, plunging them headlong into divine judgment. Finally, God's patience reaches a breaking point. The Lord has had enough of their wickedness and sets up judgment against them.

1 Samuel 2:27-36—Judgment Against Eli

Pointing forward to a time in the near future, a holy man issues a speech of judgment against Eli and his priesthood. Because Eli cannot restrain Hophni and Phinehas, and because of the seriousness of their sins, the entire priestly line of Eli is about to receive its due reward. Even the very sanctuary where Eli works is now in jeopardy of downfall. The holy man brings a frightening and tragic message. The judgment of God against it is stern and uncompromising.

Exactly who is to succeed Eli as priest is unclear from the words of the anonymous holy man. For the moment, Samuel becomes the religious leader of Israel. Later, under King David, the Zadokites fall heir to the priesthood.

1 Samuel 3—The Call of Samuel

Samuel now receives a dramatic revelation from the Lord. His special birth, his consecration into the priesthood, and his obedient service all come together in this event. God officially sanctions Samuel as a spokesman. The old era of the "judges" has ended, and a new age of divine communication with humankind has broken forth—the age of the prophet. Through Samuel, God has opened yet another door to aid Israel in her quest for salvation.

SAMUEL, A PROPHET OF THE LORD   **7**

Samuel's prophetic call is similar to those of Isaiah, Jeremiah, and Ezekiel. Three times God addresses Samuel. Samuel fails initially to recognize the identity of the speaker, thinking it is the aging Eli asking for help. But Eli quickly recognizes the experience to be holy and instructs Samuel accordingly. On the fourth address, Samuel responds invitingly, "Speak, for your servant is listening." God then responds by promising punishment for the house of Eli.

However, the message that God delivers to Samuel is not a happy one because it signals doom for Eli and his line. The message thus confirms the words spoken by the holy man. Eli's priestly reign is almost over, and his two sons are about to die. Although Samuel hesitates at first to disclose this news, Eli urges him to do as God commands. Upon hearing God's words of judgment Eli responds faithfully, "He is the LORD; let him do what is good in his eyes."

The section concludes with a statement about Samuel's increasing importance as a religious leader in early Israel (verses 19-21). His fame as a spokesman for God now extends to the limits of Israel. His priestly upbringing, now strengthened by God's call, prepares Samuel for his historic leadership of God's people. His stature as the spiritual leader of his people must now extend to the political realm, where he must answer the rising demand for a king. Thus there is little doubt within the Old Testament about Samuel's importance. He guides Israel from the time of the judges to the time of the monarchy.

DIMENSION THREE:
WHAT DOES THE BIBLE MEAN TO ME?

1 Samuel 1:1-28; 2:26—God in History

As Christians, none of us can afford to be unconcerned about the complex problems of our world. With both urban and rural crime only a fingertip away, with world hunger on the rampage, and with the rapid depletion of our world's natural resources, we must be concerned. Times were troublesome in the days of Samuel also. The final words in the Book of Judges summarize the political situation as chaotic. "In those days Israel had no king; everyone did as he saw fit."

God's word was important to the early Hebrews because it was a word that brought action—sometimes salvation and sometimes judgment. In the midst of some of Israel's darkest hours, God commissioned Samuel as a spokesman to lead the way. We as Christians confess that God is still at work in our world, directing the affairs of history. Where is God to be found amid the complex problems of our world? Who are the Samuels of today?

1 Samuel 2:1-10—Celebrating God's Reign

The ancient Hebrew religion was a religion of joy and celebration of God's mighty acts. Many of the Psalms are songs of thanksgiving where a worshiper confesses that God has come through at the eleventh hour. In the New Testament, Mary the mother of Jesus sings a similar song. (See Luke 1:46-55.) What moments in your own life have called forth such a response?

1 Samuel 2:12-17; 22-26—The Nature of Sin

Many different kinds of sin are found in the Bible—worshiping gods other than the Lord, social abuse, hypocrisy, and others. In 1 Samuel 2, Hophni and Phinehas sin by violating cultic laws. How would you define the word *sin*? What actions do you identify as sins? Are there sins for which there is no forgiveness? If so, what are those sins? How can Christians deal with sin?

The Philistines have returned the ark of the LORD (6:21).

— 2 —

The Ark of the Covenant
1 Samuel 4–6

DIMENSION ONE:
WHAT DOES THE BIBLE SAY?

Answer these questions by reading 1 Samuel 4

1. Who are the major military opponents of Israel during the days of Samuel? (4:1)

2. What symbol of God's presence encourages the Hebrews in battle? (4:3)

3. Where is the ark kept (4:3-4)

4. Why are the Philistines frightened upon learning that the ark is in the Israelite camp? (4:7-8)

5. What is the outcome of the battle? (4:10-11)

6. How does Eli learn of the outcome of the battle, and what happens to him after hearing this news? (4:12-18)

7. What does the name *Ichabod* mean? (4:21)

Answer these questions by reading 1 Samuel 5

8. Where do the Philistines take the ark? (5:1, 8, 10)

9. What happens in these cities because of the ark's presence? (5:1-12)

10. Who is the main god of the Philistines? (5:1-2)

11. What do the Philistines want to do with the ark? (5:11-12)

Answer these questions by reading 1 Samuel 6

12. How long do the Philistines have the ark? (6:1)

13. When the Philistines return the ark, what do they send along with it? Why? (6:1-6)

14. Where do they first send the ark? (6:14)

15. Why do some of the men of Beth Shemesh die? (6:19)

16. Where is the ark taken next? (6:21)

DIMENSION TWO:
WHAT DOES THE BIBLE MEAN?

1 Samuel 4:1-11—The Loss of the Ark

The opening narrative of this section reports two battles between the Israelites and the Philistines. The Philistines are non-Semitic tribes who live along the coastal plain in the southwestern part of the country. The Israelites occupy the central hill country. The books of Judges and Samuel tell of the conflicts between these two peoples, each struggling for control of the region.

The battles occur near the cities of Ebenezer and Aphek. Locate these cities on the map on page 112. They are important as guardians of Israel's heartland. To lose control of this small area would open the rest of Israel to military invasion. Thus, protecting this area is important.

The actual account of the first battle is brief, but clear: Israel loses. We read no other details about the battle. The elders of Israel then reassemble and ask, "Why did the LORD bring defeat upon us today before the Philistines?"

Israel believed that the Lord was active in her national affairs. God had been with the Israelites during the Exodus from Egypt and with persons like Joshua and Gideon. God's actions have resulted in victory in the past. When Israel lost, it meant God was displeased. (See the story of Achan in Joshua

12   1 AND 2 SAMUEL

8.) For this reason, complete obedience to God's ethical and religious demands was a necessity. So the elders of Israel wonder why the Lord permitted this defeat.

The elders quickly decide to bring the ark of the covenant to Ebenezer from its resting place at Shiloh. The priests at Shiloh are Eli and his sons, Hophni and Phinehas. The ark is box-like and can be transported by poles as if on a litter. The ark is believed to contain items of special significance to Israel's faith, such as the tablets containing the Ten Commandments. The ark is constructed in such a way that mythical creatures known as cherubim support the main section. The ark accompanies the armies of Israel in battle, and it is strange that in this particular battle it did not. The moment it arrives in camp, the Israelites are inspired and break out in joyous shouting. The noise carries all the way to the Philistine camp.

The Philistines become panicky when they realize that now Israel's powerful God has joined the battle. Their cry, "Woe to us!" is a traditional cry of mourning. Clearly they have heard of Israel's God, even if they are wrong about the details of the defeat of the Egyptians. But, they manage to contain their fears and win the second battle. It must have been a gallant battle, since they also capture the ark and kill Hophni and Phinehas. The number of Israelites actually killed has probably been exaggerated to indicate the importance of the victory.

The ark is now gone. Captured by a pagan adversary, the visual presence of the Lord is about to be removed from Israel. The army rapidly retreats. The phrase "every man fled to his tent" means that the military service has been disbanded altogether. What do these events mean for Israel? How do the people react?

1 Samuel 4:12-22—Reactions to the Loss of the Ark

Verses 12-18 describe the death of Eli. The news of the battle is delivered to the people by an anonymous Benjamite, who manages to run the nineteen miles to Shiloh in a single day. Hastening into the city, he reports the news of the defeat and the people join together in a universal cry of mourning. Torn clothing and earth on one's head are symbols of grief.

THE ARK OF THE COVENANT **13**

Due to difficulties in translating the Hebrew text, it is unclear where Eli is sitting and how he manages to miss the messenger. He is probably sitting at the entrance to the Temple. Clearly the old priest is concerned about the ark. The word translated *watching* may also mean "waiting" or "expecting." Since Eli is later described as blind, the word is best translated "expecting." The tragic news of the ark being captured is more than he can stand, and he falls over dead.

The mention of Eli being a judge over Israel is surprising, since elsewhere he is identified as a priest (1 Samuel 1:9). Also, the fact that he reigned forty years is strange since at no point in the story have we been told of his experience. Here Eli stands in the tradition of the famous judges Samson, Gideon, and Deborah. The principal religious symbol during the reign of these persons was the ark of the covenant. Thus, Eli's genuine concern for the safety of this holy object is readily understandable.

Verses 19-22 relay an account of the birth of Ichabod, the son of Phinehas. This story further attests to the sadness in Israel over the loss of the ark. With such an important object now in the hands of the enemy, dark days certainly loom ahead. The urgency of Israel's vulnerability is apparent in this brief story.

The tragic news of the death of her husband and father-in-law, and the news of the loss of the holy ark, cause Phinehas's wife to go into premature labor. Shortly after the birth of her son, she names her baby Ichabod (meaning "God's glory has departed from Israel") and dies.

Because the Hebrew text for 1 and 2 Samuel has been poorly preserved and transmitted, the details of this story are confusing. For example, the New English Bible says that the women who attended her named the baby.

1 Samuel 5—Divine Judgment Against the Philistines

The narrative now shifts back to the Philistine camp where the warriors have taken their captured booty—the Israelite ark. Historically, when one nation conquered another nation and captured its god, this was a sign of the supremacy of the conqueror's god. But not so here! The Lord of Israel has something else in mind, although neither the Philistines nor the Israelite elders seem to understand. The Lord God of Israel clearly reverses traditional thoughts about such matters, much to the surprise and misfortune of the Philistines.

The ark is taken to Ashdod, then to Gath, and then to Ekron. These cities are three of the five major Philistine cities. "Dagon's temple" refers to a Philistine temple. Dagon is a fertility god and is usually associated with grain. On the morning after the first night the ark is in the Philistine temple, the statue of Dagon is found lying face down, prostrate before the ark. Imagine the shock to the Philistines! On the second morning, Dagon's head and hands are cut off. The superiority of the Lord of Israel is clear.

Next, tumors infect the people and mice or rats invade the territory. What had originally begun as a military victory for the Philistines now turns out to be a national calamity.

Early Greek and Latin translations of this section, particularly verse 6, include a reference to a plague of mice or rats. In The Revised English Bible, verse 6 says, "The Lord's hand oppressed the people of Ashdod. He threw them into despair; he plagued them with tumours, and their territory swarmed with rats. There was death and destruction all through the city."

The tumors (or boils) could have been caused by an outbreak of bubonic plague spread by the rodents. In addition to causing the plague, mice or rats would also destroy crops and cause food shortages in the future. An infestation of mice would also explain why the Philistines sent the golden images of mice with the ark when it was returned.

The situation in Philistia worsens when the ark is moved to another city. The Philistine leaders quickly understand the significance of these events. The Lord, God of Israel, is bringing judgment against them. In verse 11, the people of Ekron ask that the ark be returned so that it will not "kill us and our people."

1 Samuel 6—The Return of the Ark

The Philistines conclude that this ark must be returned immediately. Its capture has brought disaster instead of victory. Not only must it be returned, but two offerings to God acknowledging Philistine guilt for taking the ark must be sent. The offerings are golden images of tumors and mice.

Although the Philistine leaders strongly suspect that their present predicament is the result of judgment from the God of Israel, they try to confirm their suspicions when they return the ark. They choose two milking cows to pull the cart containing the ark. If the cows complete the journey without returning to their stalls (as would ordinarily be expected), then the Lord's involvement in the disasters is confirmed. If the cows return home instead of delivering the ark, these calamities might be perceived as mere chance.

Locate Beth Shemesh on the map on page 112. This site is chosen for the return of the ark probably because it is the nearest Israelite city to the Philistine border. The Philistines could keep a close watch on the progress of the ark. The inhabitants of the village understandably rejoice at the sight of the returning ark. They assemble to offer sacrifices of thanksgiving. Perhaps in their excitement, some of the men violate the sanctity of the holy ark by peering inside. Many of the men are killed.

This section concludes in 7:1-3 with the ark being taken out of Beth Shemesh to Kiriath Jearim. It remains in Kiriath Jearim until David takes it to Jerusalem. God's sacred symbol is now back among the Israelites, and yet another crisis is resolved. As has so often been true in the stories about the judges, the Lord has turned certain defeat into victory for the people.

DIMENSION THREE:
WHAT DOES THE BIBLE MEAN TO ME?

1 Samuel 4:1-11—God's Holy Purposes

We sometimes cannot understand God's holy purposes in certain events in our lives. The Israelites evidently have the same problem. Perplexed by their initial defeat at the hands of the Philistines, the elders of Israel inquire, "Why did the LORD bring defeat to us today?" This same question would have been even more pertinent following the second defeat and the capture of the sacred ark. Why has the Lord allowed such a tragedy to befall the chosen people? Do you ask similar questions in the face of tragedy? How many times do we watch innocent persons suffer? Why does God cause or even allow such things to happen?

In the ark narrative, this original question is answered by the surprising display of divine judgment God brings upon the Philistines. God turns defeat into victory, disaster into triumph. In the midst of the crisis, no one, not even the elders of Israel, understands the full meaning of God's actions. Not until the Philistines have acknowledged God's sovereignty does that meaning become clear.

God is one who is to be trusted, respected, and obeyed. This means that the full meaning of God's purposes may not become clear until later, and we may have to live with uncertainty. But uncertainty is the essence of trust. Just as do the elders of Israel, we must learn to wait and trust in the power and benevolent will of God. This trust is imbedded deep within the nature of faith.

1 Samuel 5—God's Awesome Power

For some Christians today, the terrifying nature and actions of God in the Old Testament are difficult to reconcile with the loving Father as shown through Jesus Christ. The awesome and powerful God who brings wrath upon offenders of divine law and opponents of the people may well seem foreign indeed. In this narrative about the ark, God's display of power is unleashed first against the unsuspecting Philistines, then against the men of Beth Shemesh for a religious offense. The Philistines feel the sting of God's power on more than one occasion during these years of the judges. Where else in the Old Testament is God's power demonstrated in a frightening or terrifying manner?

To understand the Bible we must look beneath the fantastic stories and consider what is the deeper point. God's awesomeness and power are not meant to evoke fear, but rather to solicit trust, confidence, and respect. The God of Israel, like the God of Jesus and Paul, is a God that humanity can trust and respect. God intervenes on behalf of true believers. By probing deeper into the Old Testament narratives we can narrow the gap between the God of the ancient Hebrews and the God of Jesus.

Appoint a king to lead us,
such as all the other nations have (8:5).

—— 3 ——
The People Ask for a King
1 Samuel 7–10

DIMENSION ONE:
WHAT DOES THE BIBLE SAY?

Answer these questions by reading 1 Samuel 7

1. What does Samuel tell the Israelites they must do to return to the Lord? (7:3-4)

2. How is the Philistine army defeated at Mizpah? (7:10)

3. What is Samuel's occupation? (7:15-17)

Answer these questions by reading 1 Samuel 8

4. Who are Joel and Abijah? (8:2)

5. When Samuel's sons are judges, what do they do? (8:3)

6. Why do the elders want a king? (8:5)

7. How does Samuel feel about their request for a king? (8:6)

8. What does the Lord tell Samuel to do? (8:7-9)

9. What does Samuel say a king might do? (8:10-17)

10. Do the people change their minds? (8:19-20)

Answer these questions by reading 1 Samuel 9

11. Who is Kish? (9:1-2)

12. How does Saul happen to meet Samuel? (9:3-14)

13. Why does Samuel recognize Saul? (9:15-16)

Answer these questions by reading 1 Samuel 10

14. What does Samuel tell Saul? (10:1)

15. What happens to Saul when the spirit of God enters him? (10:6, 9-11)

16. How does Samuel choose Saul as king? (10:20-24)

17. Where is Saul? (10:22)

18. Where is Saul's home? (10:26)

DIMENSION TWO:
WHAT DOES THE BIBLE MEAN?

1 Samuel 7—Samuel as Judge

Verses 1 and 2 actually complete the ark narrative from Chapters 4–6. Once the ark has been returned to Israel, joy and peace return to the land. A priest, Eleazar, is consecrated to care for the ark. The ark will remain at Kiriath Jearim until David takes it to Jerusalem.

Verses 3 and 4 report a major sin among the Israelites—the sin of disloyalty to the Lord. They were worshiping other gods. Among the more prominent Canaanite gods occasionally worshiped by Israel are the Baals (lords of the land) and the Ashtareths (female counterparts of the Baals). These gods and goddesses were revered by the Canaanites in local fertility cults. The purpose of such worship was to insure the continued fertility of the soil so that crops would prosper. The temptation to adopt Canaanite religion, along with Canaanite agricultural practices, was strong in early Israel. But under Samuel's leadership, Israel strongly resisted worshiping other gods and remained faithful to the Lord.

Verses 5-16 describe God's miraculous intervention to rescue Israel from a Philistine attack. All Israel has gathered at Mizpah to participate in a national ceremony of purification. When the Philistines learn of the assembly, they prepare to do battle. Israel is understandably frightened and pleads with Samuel to pray to God on her behalf. Samuel offers a burnt offering to the Lord. God responds positively by causing thunder that confuses the Philistines. Israel then pursues the enemy as far as the border. Samuel erects a monument there called the Ebenezer stone to celebrate the victory. Once again, peace prevails across Israel.

Samuel is the last of the group of judges who ruled Israel during the twelfth and eleventh centuries B.C. His travels from place to place, his prayers that bring divine intervention, and his fame as an arbiter link him historically with Samson, Gideon, Deborah, and the other judges of the Old Testament. The activity of these persons clearly unite religious, military, and judicial functions in early Israel.

1 Samuel 8—Israel Asks for a King

Possibly ten or twenty years have passed between 7:15-17 and Chapter 8:1-3. By now, Samuel is an old man, and has given some of his duties to his sons, Joel and Abijah. Beersheba, an important outpost in Israel's security network and the site of a major religious sanctuary, is in the southern part of Palestine. Obviously, Samuel's sphere of influence covers a substantial area.

In verses 4 and 5, we are told that the elders come to Samuel and ask that he name a king. The elders are the leaders of the different tribes in early Israel. From their perspective, the present system of government in Israel is unsatisfactory. Samuel is too old and his sons are corrupt.

Later, in verse 20, the people suggest military leadership as another reason for the change to monarchy. In a sense, their point is well taken. Kingship might provide a stronger and better regulated military force. However, Samuel points out that the disadvantages far outweigh the advantages of kingship. Kings are more appropriate to pagan nations than to God's chosen people.

As is proper for a man of his piety, Samuel prays about their request for a king. God responds by instructing Samuel to proceed with the appointment of a king. But first he tells Samuel he must warn the people of the potential dangers in having a king. The Lord also tells Samuel that the elders' request for a king is not a rejection of his leadership, but in truth an act of disloyalty to God.

Samuel outlines the possible abuses under the reign of a monarch. The king may take away people's land as well as their crops. He may force subjects to serve in his army, on his royal farms, and in his palace. And once the king is in power, he is all but impossible to remove.

Nevertheless, the elders persist in their demand for a king. The Lord instructs Samuel a second time to abide by their wishes. So, in order to make appropriate plans, Samuel sends them home.

1 Samuel 9:1–10:16—Saul, the Lord's Anointed King

The genealogy in 9:1 is the Bible's way of calling our attention to the prestige of Saul's family. A well-respected family, great wealth, and striking physical appearance all suggest a man favored by God.

The famous holy man (9:6), who turns out to be Samuel, is a type of professional religious leader. This person is to assist persons in discerning God's will. Holy men were often called *seers* because of their visual revelations. They were thought to possess special powers enabling them to see God's mysterious power or allay the spirits of evil. They could offer advice on many problems, such as marriage, war, God, children, and lost articles.

Samuel's anointing of Saul symbolizes God's bestowal of divine power. God's spirit enters him and strengthens him for special service. From the point of view of the Old Testament, Israel's leaders drew their power and authority to rule from God. With God's help, a leader could work wonders, as Samuel, Saul, and David illustrate.

Prophets (like those mentioned in 10:10) usually moved around from place to place in groups rather than locating permanently at a single religious center. These prophets work themselves into an emotional frenzy and sing, dance, and utter all types of pronouncements. They are known as ecstatic bands due to their efforts to prophesy while in an emotional state of ecstasy. They were often frowned upon by the religious leaders in Israel. For Saul to join such a strange group, even momentarily, is unusual behavior. Thus, a proverb developed to describe anyone engaging in unusual behavior: "Is Saul also among the prophets?"

1 Samuel 10:17-27—Saul, King by Elimination

With Saul having been anointed a prince over Israel, it is surprising to discover a second ceremony in which Saul is crowned king. This second account is a continuation of the narrative begun in Chapter 8, where both God and Samuel are opposed to kingship.

Shortly after Samuel's dismissal of Israel (see 8:22), he reconvenes the people at Mizpah. Samuel presents another speech contrasting God's past goodness to the Israelites with their faithlessness. His point is that monarchy is actually divine judgment rather than a blessing.

Compare Samuel's speech here with the one in 8:7-9. Notice that both speeches refer to the exodus tradition as of special importance. Miraculous leadership in Egypt shows God to be Lord of all peoples and giver of life to the covenant people. The Exodus is central in Israel's main confessions of faith (Deuteronomy 26; Joshua 24). Thus, in these two speeches, the Lord reminds Israel of who she is and who is her God. Why then does she need a king? Israel does not trust God when she demands a ruler other than the Lord.

To select a king, the Israelites are marched before Samuel, tribe by tribe, clan by clan, family by family, man by man. As each one passes, they are eliminated one by one until one is selected. Saul, of the family of Matri, is chosen.

The word *baggage* in 10:22 literally means *gear* or *equipment*. It can refer to domestic ware, military equipment, or religious paraphernalia. Also, the reason for his hiding is unclear. Some scholars have suggested Saul hid due to modesty or shyness. Perhaps Saul, from the humblest of families (9:21), is reluctant to take the great office of king.

Saul's physical size is again emphasized here. He towers over the Israelites by twelve to sixteen inches. Despite God's initial misgivings about naming a king, Saul is a divine choice. Shouts of joy and celebration announce the Israelites' devotion to their new leader. Samuel then instructs Saul on the rights and duties of kingship. Monarchy begins in Israel. A new form of leadership has been born among God's chosen people. Israel has a king.

DIMENSION THREE:
WHAT DOES THE BIBLE MEAN TO ME?

1 Samuel 8:10-22—Church and State

The separation of church and state is a basic right guaranteed to each American by the Constitution. Government (local, state, or national) in the United States has no right to dictate belief or practice, unless such matters violate other laws. By the same token, institutionalized religion has no legal right to control the state. No denomination or congregation can declare war or pass laws. In our American system, church and state are constitutionally separated.

This section in 1 Samuel on the rise of kingship raises the issue of church and state in an interesting way. Can the older type of leadership under the judges continue to provide guidance for an emerging nation? Or is a stronger, better-organized, centralized authority needed? Certainly, the Lord is active in the selection process in both accounts. God's providential leadership continues, but the human ruler now changes from a professional religious leader to a political figure. This uneasy tension between God's rule and the activities of the king gives rise to some serious problems later in Israel's history.

The problem of church-state relations comes to focus for us in the matter of how the church expresses itself in governmental matters. Perhaps Christians must voice their opinions on political matters individually rather than through the church.

Some issues for class discussion are (1) prayer in public schools, (2) holidays for Easter and Christmas, (3) "In God We Trust" on U.S. coinage, and (4) lobbying efforts of religious groups to elect political candidates.

1 Samuel 10:9-13—The Gift of God's Spirit

The experience of the indwelling of God's Spirit is called *charismatic endowment*. This divine power empowers Israel's early leaders such as Moses, Joshua, Samuel, Saul, and David. In the New Testament, this power comes to the disciples of Pentecost.

Many Christians today who claim to have experienced the Spirit are also practicing *glossolalia*, or speaking in tongues. Moreover, they argue that without the gift of the Spirit, which they equate with speaking in tongues, a person's soul is not truly in harmony with God. Caution is needed here, as well as love and tolerance on both sides. God's Spirit manifests itself in many forms. Glossolalia is not the only evidence of God's Spirit.

Read 1 Corinthians 12–14. What are other gifts of God's Spirit? How is God's Spirit manifest in your life?

So all the people went to Gilgal and confirmed Saul
as king in the presence of the LORD (11:15).

—— 4 ——
The Kingship of Saul
1 Samuel 11–15

DIMENSION ONE:
WHAT DOES THE BIBLE SAY?

Answer the questions by reading 1 Samuel 11

1. Which Israelite town does Nahash the Ammonite threaten? (11:1)

2. What terms does Nahash offer the men of Jabesh Gilead? (11:2)

3. How does Saul respond to this crisis? (11:11)

4. What does Samuel do after Saul's victory at Jabesh? (11:14-15)

Answer these questions by reading 1 Samuel 12

5. What do the people say to Samuel? (12:4)

6. What does Samuel remind the people that the Lord has done? (12:7-8)

7. What was Israel's sin during this period, and how did the Lord respond? (12:9-12)

8. What conditions does God give for Israel to obtain continued blessing? (12:14)

9. What will happen if Israel and her king do not abide by these terms? (12:25)

Answer these questions by reading 1 Samuel 13

10. Who are the opponents of Saul and the Israelites during this period? (13:4)

11. Why does Saul proceed with the sacrificial offerings at Gilgal? (13:11-12)

12. How does Samuel react to Saul's deeds at Gilgal? (13:13)

13. Why do the Hebrews have so few metal weapons to use in their wars against the Philistines? (13:19)

Answer these questions by reading 1 Samuel 14

14. How is Jonathan related to Saul? (14:1)

15. How does Jonathan characterize the non-Semitic Philistines? (14:6)

16. Who is Ahijah and what role does he play in the Saul stories? (14:3, 18)

17. What is Saul's oath during this period of warfare? (14:24)

18. Which Israelite does not follow Saul's oath? (14:27)

19. How does Saul learn that Jonathan has violated the oath? (14:41-42)

20. How does Jonathan escape death for his sin? (14:45)

21. Who are Saul's family members? (14:49-51)

Answer these questions by reading 1 Samuel 15

22. What does Saul spare in the battle with the Amalekites? (15:9)

23. What excuse does Saul offer Samuel for this act of disobedience? (15:21)

24. How does the Lord react to Saul's sin? (15:35)

DIMENSION TWO:
WHAT DOES THE BIBLE MEAN?

1 Samuel 11—Saul's Victory at Jabesh Gilead

Two principal events occur in this chapter: (1) Saul wins an important military victory over the Ammonites, and (2) Saul is publicly proclaimed king. Remember that Saul has already been crowned king before all Israel at Mizpah (10:24). Perhaps the present story is a continuation of 10:16, where Saul has been named prince privately but Samuel tells him to say nothing about it. Here, his selection is justified by a military victory and made public.

This chapter introduces Nahash the Ammonite as Saul's opponent. The territory of Ammon lies east of the Jordan. The borders of Ammon touch the borders of the Hebrew tribes of Gad and Reuben. Conflicts over these borders characterize the relations between Ammon and Israel during the early part of Saul's reign.

The word *treaty* (11:1) may also be translated *covenant*. A treaty implies a mutual agreement satisfactory to both parties, even though one party may be superior to the other. Both participants have mutual rights and obligations, but each group retains its integrity. However, here Nahash flaunts tradition. He offers the men of Jabesh two unsatisfactory alternatives: death or loss of their right eyes. He clearly wishes to humiliate Israel during her moment of weakness. But he does not count on Saul!

Saul moves quickly after learning by chance the plight of Jabesh. Empowered by the Spirit of God (verse 6), Saul assembles an army. The dismembering of an animal and its distribution functions as a direct order for men to bear arms. The army marches north for a three-pronged assault against Nahash and the Ammonites. Saul and his forces rout the enemy, and a humiliating crisis for the Israelites is averted.

Along with Samuel, all Israel then gathers at Gilgal to proclaim Saul king. By virtue of his excellent military leadership at Jabesh, Saul is the choice by universal accord. But, he is also king because God endows him with divine spirit. As long as Saul is obedient to the Lord's commands, his kingship is secure and his power and authority are firm. But, this situation is short-lived, as we shall soon discover.

1 Samuel 12—Samuel's Address to Israel

Chapter 12 begins with Samuel's oath of innocence. Such an oath attests to his spiritual and moral leadership among the Israelites and to his integrity as a leader. He points to his sensitivity to the needs and wishes of the people, including their request to appoint a king. In all matters, Samuel has been a faithful servant to the Lord. But now, leadership has passed from his hands to the office of the king. God has ordained a new form of leadership for the people.

Samuel now presents a brief review of God's saving acts on behalf of Israel (12:6-18). Here he follows a set pattern: (1) Israel abandons her faith in the Lord, (2) the Lord allows her adversaries to plunder Israel, (3) Israel confesses her sins to God, and (4) the Lord empowers a leader to free Israel from her oppressors.

Samuel concludes his address with a final admonition to fear the Lord; otherwise, disastrous consequences are certain to follow. The Lord rewards those who are faithful and punishes those who are disobedient. The transition from judge to king is now complete. Samuel turns over the reigns of authority to Saul, and a new era in the history of Israel begins.

1 Samuel 13—4—Saul's Warfare With the Philistines

To understand Saul's military encounter with the Philistines during this period, locate the following sites on the map on page 112: Micmash, Geba, Gibeah, and Gilgal. These cities are all located in the hill country. This is rugged terrain, dotted by caves, dry steam beds (wadis), and craggy hills.

The age of Saul when he began to rule Israel is omitted. The biblical writer was understandably confused. In 9:2, Saul appears as a youthful son of Kish. In 11:5, he is a grown man who musters an army and defeats Nahash. In 14:1, he has a grown son. The chronology of Saul's reign is difficult for us to establish. Evidently, it was no easier for the biblical writer.

The account of the battles is easier to describe. At this time, the Philistines dominated the central hill country of Ephraim. When Jonathan launches a surprising and successful attack against a Philistine camp at Geba, the Philistines respond by assembling their troops and marching to Micmash, overlooking the Israelite camp. Israel panics and flees in all directions.

For a time, the Philistines control the area by frequent raiding parties and by depriving the Israelites of metal weapons. Then in a second surprise attack by Jonathan, the Philistine watchmen are slain. The Philistines now begin to flee, with

Saul's army in hot pursuit. Only an untimely violation of Saul's oath to fast spares the Philistines from a complete rout.

The mention of the ephod (14:3) and the ark of God (14:18) is important to the overall understanding of this story. The ephod is a rectangular medallion possibly worn by a priest around his neck. It contains the Urim and Thummin, the sacred lot. This ephod is different from the little waistcloth worn by Samuel (2:18). The priest wearing this object is a certain Ahijah, a distant relative of Eli. Ahijah's presence suggests that the events of the day are to be understood as within the providential actions of the Lord.

In verse 24, Saul proclaims a fast. He hopes to please the Lord with this action. However, the oath turns out to be poor judgment. An army weakened by hunger is scarcely able to fight. Even worse, the innocent violator of the oath is none other than Jonathan, Saul's son. This episode concludes with Jonathan being ransomed for his sin. Even so, an ominous cloud has been cast over Saul's house.

1 Samuel 13:7-15; 15:1-35—Saul's Disobedience

Although 13:7b-15a is out of sequence here, we chose to place it alongside another account of Saul's disobedience. The narrative in 13:7b-15a interrupts the story of Saul's war with the Philistines. Possibly the mention of Gilgal in verse 8 led the final editor to insert another Gilgal story immediately following this narrative. Also this brief episode further emphasizes Saul's inadequacies as a king.

The seven-day wait refers to 10:8 where Samuel has told the newly anointed prince to proceed to Gilgal and wait for him. Saul waits in anticipation, and his troops begin to desert him. Before engaging the Philistines, he feels he must invoke God's blessing. He can wait for Samuel no longer, so he offers the sacrifice himself. When Samuel finally arrives, he is enraged at Saul's hasty behavior and informs him that this action will cost him the kingship.

Saul's disobedience described in Chapter 15 is much more contemptible than in the previous account. While both deeds result in the Lord's judgment against Saul, only the second account presents an offense that justifies the extreme punishment that Saul receives. Saul is sent to annihilate the Amalekites. Although he defeats them in battle, he spares King Agag and their choicest animals. This willful act of disobedience is detected and denounced by Samuel. Saul has intentionally violated God's word. The office of kingship will soon pass into other hands.

The Amalekites were a tribe of Bedouins who lived south of Canaan. In the Old Testament they are perennial enemies of Israel. The Kenites are also a Bedouin tribe located south of Canaan. But since they befriended the invading Israelites on their march north from Sinai, and because of their associations with Moses (Judges 1:16), Saul excuses them.

This chapter portrays Saul as a victorious king who has considerable military ability. Unfortunately, he is taken in by popular opinion and ill-informed about what to do with booty taken during war. Once the Lord has placed an adversary under a ban, everything must be destroyed. Saul does not do this, and no excuse is sufficient.

DIMENSION THREE: WHAT DOES THE BIBLE MEAN TO ME?

1 Samuel 12:6-18—Divine Retribution

Retribution is the idea that God rewards the righteous person and punishes the wicked person. Many religions, both ancient and modern, affirm this notion. The concept of retribution provides guidance and incentive for our daily conduct and stresses the importance of proper behavior. Many times the relationship between cause and effect in human conduct is both knowable and predictable. But in the worlds of Samuel and Jesus, this relationship has a third dimension—God. Illness, military defeat, prosperity, and progeny are the direct results of God's blessing or punishment. In this section, Samuel lays out God's expectations of Israel. If she follows God's words obediently, then she will prosper. If she disobeys, then God will punish her. The same obligation is laid also upon

Israel's king. The future of Israel and her king depends on strict observance of God's commands.

Retribution is not a simple concept in the Bible. Neither is it simple today. What are some instances of divine punishment or blessing in your life?

1 Samuel 13:8-15—Obedience to God

In this passage Samuel explains the requirements of the Lord, and he places before the people their alternatives. Obedience to God's commandments leads to blessing and prosperity, but disobedience leads to punishment. But what exactly does God expect Israel to obey? Here the reference is to the laws of Moses, especially the Ten Commandments. God wants absolute loyalty and trust from the people and their king. God sets forth the guidelines, and then sends prophets to help the people understand them. Obedience is not only possible; it is expected.

Few Christians today would dispute this demand for obedience to God's laws. For many of us the problem is understanding exactly what God demands. Are the ancient laws of Moses in the Old Testament binding for us? Do Jesus' teachings about personal wealth and submission to ancient cultural norms apply to us today? How can we choose among the many Christian voices calling for our allegiance?

David came to Saul and
entered his service (16:21).

—— 5 ——
David's Early Years
1 Samuel 16–20

DIMENSION ONE:
WHAT DOES THE BIBLE SAY?

Answer these questions by reading 1 Samuel 16

1. Why does Samuel visit Jesse the Bethlehemite? (16:1)

2. What does Samuel tell the elders of Bethlehem? (16:5)

3. How does the Lord know which person is to be king? (16:7)

4. Who does Samuel anoint as king? (16:13)

5. How does David receive God's power? (16:13)

6. What happens to Saul when the Spirit of the Lord leaves him? (16:14)

7. How do Saul's attendants treat his illness? (16:18-23)

Answer these questions by reading 1 Samuel 17

8. Who comes from the Philistine army to challenge the Israelite army? (17:4)

9. Who are David's three eldest brothers and what do they do? (17:13)

10. Why does Jesse send David to his brothers? (17:17-18)

11. What rewards does Saul offer anyone who kills Goliath? (17:25)

12. Why doesn't Saul want David to fight Goliath? (17:33)

13. How does David refute Saul's objections? (17:36-37)

14. What does David carry with him to meet Goliath? (17:40)

15. What does David say his victory over Goliath will prove? (17:47)

16. What does David do to the fallen Philistine? (17:51)

17. Who is Abner? (17:55)

Answer these questions by reading 1 Samuel 18

18. What is Jonathan's attitude toward David? (18:1)

19. Why does Saul's initial affection for David change? (18:8-9)

20. Why does Saul present David with Michal, his daughter? (18:20-25)

Answer these questions by reading 1 Samuel 19

21. Apart from jealousy, for what other reason does Saul attempt to kill David? (19:9)

22. How does Michal help David escape? (19:13-14)

23. Who does David join at Ramah? (19:18)

24. What happens to Saul as he enters Naioth? (19:23-24)

Answer these questions by reading 1 Samuel 20

25. What does Jonathan learn that Saul intends to do? (20:33)

26. What does Jonathan tell David to do? (20:42)

DIMENSION TWO:
WHAT DOES THE BIBLE MEAN?

1 Samuel 16—David Enters Saul's Court

In Chapter 16, we become acquainted with David in two separate narratives. First, we meet him as the unanticipated choice of God as king. Second, he appears as an able warrior and a skilled musician who soothes Saul's depression. The historical relationship between these two accounts is not clear. Certainly it is surprising that David's anointing (16:13) is apparently unknown to Saul or to any member of his court. Despite these historical problems, the two stories compliment each another. In both accounts, David is introduced as an appealing figure who has the Spirit of God. There can be no doubt that he is the man God has chosen to be the eventual ruler of the people.

After reviewing seven of the sons of Jesse, Samuel fails to receive the Lord's word that any of these is the one who will be king. So Samuel inquires if Jesse has other sons, and he does. David, the youngest, is summoned, and much to the surprise of all, he is the one with God's approval. Samuel then anoints him, and David instantly receives the Spirit of God. He is now equipped for service.

In the second narrative, David appears as a brave young warrior who also is skilled at playing the harp. He is brought into Saul's court to play for the king during Saul's moments of depression. Notice the very flattering way David is described: he "knows how to play the harp. He is a brave man and a warrior, He speaks well and is a fine-looking man." Most important, David stands in God's favor: "The LORD is with him." Few figures in the Old Testament receive such laudatory introductions. David is everything Saul could expect a person to be. It is little wonder that David instantly wins Saul's affection and then achieves national popularity.

1 Samuel 17—David Kills Goliath

The exact site of David's great victory over Goliath is difficult to determine. Most scholars locate Socoh about fourteen miles west of Bethlehem, in the direction of Philistine territory. This passage mentions a valley between the two armies. The valleys in this region are important for military reasons as well as for agricultural and pastoral pursuits.

Goliath was a person of tremendous height compared to the average Israelite who was probably less than six feet tall.

The heavy armor he wore must have been impressive to the more poorly-equipped Israelites. Bronze was not generally available to Saul's army. Also, Goliath was almost totally covered by armor. His vulnerability is at a minimum.

In contrast to Goliath, David appears as a young shepherd who has come to resupply his brothers with provisions. His only combat experience has been with bears and lions attacking the sheep. When he volunteers to meet the pagan challenger, everyone is shocked. Who, David? But David's great faith in the Lord calms their doubts, and he goes forth valiantly armed with only a sling and five small stones. One swing from the sling and Goliath falls to the ground.

David runs forward and uses the Philistine's own sword to behead him. The giant has fallen. The Lord has once again conquered a mighty foe with a small, but devoted, servant. The Philistine threat dissipates once again, and their army scatters in disarray. Now all Israel knows that David is the one upon whom the Spirit of the Lord has come. He is a national hero, and moves into Saul's company, winning his confidence and the loyalty of Jonathan, Saul's son.

1 Samuel 18—Saul's Jealousy of David

This chapter describes one of the classic friendships of the Old Testament, that between Jonathan and David. The king's son is so drawn and attached to the poor but brave shepherd that he bestows his own clothing and weaponry upon him. A covenant of loyalty binds them together. Jonathan willingly acknowledges David's superiority. There is no hint of envy or jealousy between these two persons, only a genuine respect and loyalty. The relationship is based on mutual trust and respect.

In 18:8, Saul becomes jealous of David's success and makes plans to assassinate him or have him killed by the Philistines. But all Saul's plans to destroy David fail. David is truly a man protected by God, and destined to become king. Saul is depicted as a pathetic figure clawing to retain his throne. His best-laid plans always seem to backfire. His desperation intensifies as time passes.

1 Samuel 19—Saul Attempts to Kill David

Saul's jealousy of David now erupts into a succession of futile attempts on his life. David's increasing popularity, along with Saul's rages of despair, form a vivid contrast in the development of these two characters. Saul's downward plunge continues, and David's rise to prominence intensifies.

After fleeing to Samuel at Ramah, David withstands four attempts to capture him, the last by Saul himself. Saul and his army are thrown into ecstatic states of confusion and begin acting in abnormal ways. The Bible attributes Saul's behavior to an evil spirit that had come from God (19:9).

The image mentioned in 19:13 probably refers to a small statue found in many ancient homes. These statues were very important possessions, since their presence induced the blessings of the god. Apparently, the one kept in Michal and David's home was almost of human size since it deceived Saul's soldiers.

1 Samuel 20—David and Jonathan

The concluding chapter in this lesson describes David's departure from Saul's court with a fond farewell from Jonathan. David, mystified by Saul's hostility toward him, enlists Jonathan's aid to determine the cause. Jonathan still finds it difficult to believe that his father harbors animosity toward such a loyal and trustworthy servant as David. The two friends develop a plan to discover Saul's real feeling toward David. Unfortunately, David's worst suspicions are true. Saul seeks his death. As agreed, a servant shoots an arrow beyond David, warning him of danger. Then, he and Jonathan reaffirm their loyalty to one another and part ways.

David bids farewell to Saul's court for the final time. He now becomes a fugitive, seeking shelter first at one place and then another. It will be interesting to follow David's adventures across Israel and Judah. How will God direct affairs so that David eventually succeeds Saul? Such destiny seems now very remote. Now David must literally run for his life!

DIMENSION THREE:
WHAT DOES THE BIBLE MEAN TO ME?

1 Samuel 17:31-54—The Weak Humble the Strong

The Bible goes to great lengths to contrast the young inexperienced shepherd with the mighty warrior. Both Goliath's size and his armor should have discouraged anyone. But David, confident of the Lord's help, bravely assailed the pagan foe, and won. The Lord humbled the strong by means of the weak. This theme is repeated many times in the Bible from Genesis to Revelation.

As members of God's community, we must acknowledge the sovereignty of divine power. The ultimate power in history is the Lord. Our trust must reside in God's will, not in our own systems of security. But trusting in the Lord is not the same as urging idle pacifism. David marched forth to meet the warrior. We also must confront the powers of evil in our world. The difference is in our ultimate trust. Our strength and courage come from the Lord. Victory comes to the person whose faith is strong.

1 Samuel 19:8-24—Evil Spirits

To many Christians the notion of evil spirits is theologically offensive and scientifically questionable. How can a loving and compassionate God inflict suffering on persons? Are not Saul's punishments disproportionate to his offenses? Are evil spirits compatible with a twentieth-century world? Why or why not?

The Bible's perspective is vastly different from ours. In describing Saul's illness the Bible makes a theological interpretation, not a psychological evaluation. To recognize this difference in perspective is useful to modern Christians. We need not abandon our trust in science or question the value of psychology. We must remember that theology is a matter of faith, and it places ultimate trust in a supreme power.

1 Samuel 20:35-42—The Quality of Relationships

Few better models of deep, abiding friendship exist in the Bible than between Jonathan and David. The ultimate outcome of this relationship helps us understand it better now. Saul's jealousy drives him to desperation and instability. He finally commits suicide. Jonathan and David draw strength and courage from their relationship, even to the very end. In this relationship there is no place for mistrust or malice. Jonathan accepts David's destiny with a sense of peace and good tidings. Not even Saul's reminder to Jonathan that his succession is in jeopardy provokes his anger toward David (20:30-31).

Human relationships are the backbone of good emotional health. Many psychologists tell us that a major cause of personal unhappiness is the inability to establish and maintain relationships. People are social creatures, made for life with others. Homes are broken and marriages dissolved because of unhappy relationships.

Look around you and count the number of persons suffering from loneliness, hostility, and insecurity. When we are unable to have deep and meaningful relationships, our sense of personhood suffers. How can we learn to relate better to each other? What does the relationship between Jonathan and David tell us about our relationships to others?

Day after day Saul searched for him,
but God did not give David into his hands (23:14).

— 6 —

David and Saul

1 Samuel 21–26

DIMENSION ONE:
WHAT DOES THE BIBLE SAY?

Answer these questions by reading 1 Samuel 21

1. Who is the priest at Nob? (21:1)

2. What request does David make of Ahimelech? (21:3)

3. How does Ahimelech respond to this request? (21:4-6)

4. Who else observes the exchange between David and Ahimelech? (21:7)

5. What additional item does Ahimelech give to David? (21:8-9)

6. How does Achish, king of Gath, react to David's visit and his strange behavior? (21:14-15)

Answer these questions by reading 1 Samuel 22

7. Who joins David while he is hiding in the cave of Adullam? (22:1-2)

8. Why does David visit the king of Moab? (22:3)

9. What information does Doeg furnish King Saul (22:9-10)

10. As a result of his aid to David, what happens to Ahimelech and his priestly family? (22:18-20)

Answer these questions by reading 1 Samuel 23

11. What threat prompts David's intervention at Keilah? (23:1)

12. How does David learn what the citizens of Keilah will do if he remains there? (23:9-12)

13. Who meets David at Horesh to offer him encouragement and support? (23:16)

14. What prevents Saul from capturing David in the Desert of Maon? (23:26-27)

Answer these questions by reading 1 Samuel 24

15. Why is David unable to kill Saul when he has an opportunity? (24:6)

16. What evidence does David offer Saul of his innocence of treason or wrongdoing? (24:11)

17. How does Saul react to David's words? (24:16-17)

Answer these questions by reading 1 Samuel 25

18. What famous leader dies, and where is he buried? (25:1)

19. Why does David feel justified in requesting provisions from Nabal? (25:7)

20. How does Nabal respond to David's request? (25:10-11)

21. How does Abigail resolve this dispute? (25:25-27)

22. As a consequence of her kindness to David, what happens to Abigail? (25:40-42)

Answer these questions by reading 1 Samuel 26

23. How does Saul learn where David is hiding? (26:1)

24. What do David and Abishai do to Saul? (26:12)

25. How does David use Saul's spear and his water jug? (26:15-16)

26. What does Saul say to David after hearing his declaration of innocence? (26:21)

DIMENSION TWO:
WHAT DOES THE BIBLE MEAN?

1 Samuel 21—David on the Run

The first part of this chapter is a narrative about David's visit to the sanctuary at Nob and Ahimelech, its priest. To allay Ahimelech's fears about helping a fugitive, David says he is on a royal errand and needs supplies. The priest complies reluctantly, since he has only consecrated bread left. David also repossesses Goliath's sword, which had evidently been placed there following the death of the Philistine warrior. This entire transaction is witnessed by Doeg, one of Saul's soldiers. Unfortunately, Doeg has a good memory.

Nob is located a few miles north of Jerusalem, in the territory of Benjamin. The city is thus very close to Gibeah, Saul's home. The priest at this sanctuary is Ahimelech, a distant relative of Eli, the former priest at Shiloh.

The consecrated bread mentioned in verse 4 is the bread of the Presence (Leviticus 24:5-9) that is placed on a table inside the Temple. It is reserved for the priests, or at least those who are pure in a cultic sense. Jesus refers to this incident (Matthew 12:3-4), and suggests that David was correct in placing human needs above cultic regulations.

Doeg is not an Israelite. He is from Edom, a small country southeast of Judah. His presence in Saul's army indicates Saul may have been using foreign mercenary soldiers. Doeg later recalls what he saw at Nob, and fuels Saul's wrath against the holy place and its priesthood.

The ephod mentioned in verse 9 is a priestly garment, perhaps like that worn by the young Samuel (2:18). This ephod is not the box containing the sacred objects, Urim and Thummim.

The second incident in this chapter tells of an encounter between David and Achish, king of Gath. Gath is a Philistine city southwest of Jerusalem. It is one of five major Philistine cities. Its king, Achish, recognizes David as an Israelite leader and a mighty warrior. His servants refer to the popular song celebrating David's victories. Just as with the incident at Nob,

David's quick wit enables him to overcome a potentially threatening situation—he feigns madness.

1 Samuel 22—The Slaughter at Nob

The major part of Chapter 22 tells of Saul's slaughter of the priests at Nob. From Doeg, the Edomite, Saul learns that Ahimelech provided aid to David. Such an act is treason, and is punishable by death. But none of Saul's soldiers are willing to participate in the killing of holy men, except the Edomite. This scoundrel willingly and enthusiastically slays eighty-five priests, plus many more persons from the city. Only Abiathar escapes and flees to David for safety.

This brutal treatment of the Lord's priests severs all contact between Saul and God. He is now without a priesthood to serve as a link to the Lord. In fact, all the priests of the Lord are dead except Abiathar, who now, ironically, serves David. It is David who preserves the priestly family and stands in God's favor. Abiathar will continue to serve David during his fugitive days and during his reign as king.

David's connection to the Lord is secured in this otherwise bloody and tragic episode. Yet David, too, must share some of the responsibility for the affair at Nob. Had he not lied to Abiathar about his mission, Abiathar would probably not have aided David willingly.

1 Samuel 23:1-13—David Rescues Keilah

This episode recounts David's valiant defense of the city of Keilah. Keilah is located northwest of Hebron. Like so many of the cities David visits during his fugitive days, Keilah is in Judah, David's home territory. David serves as a general protector of this area and has the support and respect of the citizenry.

Once David has subdued the Philistine threat, Saul moves quickly to capture him while he is still within the walls of Keilah. David calls upon Abiathar and the priest consults the ephod to determine God's will. They learn of Saul's plan and manage to escape just before Saul arrives.

The meaning of this brief story is clear. The Lord is protecting David by means of Abiathar, the priest. By safeguarding the priest of the Lord, David secures his favored place before the Lord. On the other hand, Saul can do nothing right because he lacks communication with the Lord.

1 Samuel 23:14–24:22—Saul Pursues David

In 23:19-29, David narrowly escapes Saul's clutches. The Ziphites inform Saul where David is hiding, and Saul quickly moves his troops to surround him. Trapped in a squeeze from both sides of the mountain, David's small forces are in trouble. Suddenly a messenger appears and tells Saul of a Philistine attack elsewhere. Saul withdraws his troops, and David is spared.

Chapter 24 relates the story of how David spares Saul's life. In hot pursuit of his foe, Saul goes aside for a moment into a cave. It happens that David and some of his men are hiding in that very cave. At an opportune moment, David approaches Saul, but instead of killing him, he merely cuts off part of his robe. David uses this act to demonstrate his good faith and loyalty to Saul. Saul acknowledges David's innocence and confirms his right to rule Israel and establish a dynasty.

1 Samuel 25—David and Abigail

This chapter tells of David's relationship with the beautiful and intelligent Abigail. The plot of the chapter is simple and direct. Nabal is a wealthy member of the Calebite tribe in southern Judah. David sends messengers to request provisions from Nabal, partly on the basis of protection David has offered him. Nabal refuses and treats David's men rudely. David is outraged at Nabal's bad manners and his lack of gratitude, and so he prepares for an assault to teach Nabal a lesson.

When Nabal's wife learns of David's plan, she quickly assembles provisions and hurries to intercept David. Impressed with her charm, her wisdom, and her gifts, David calls off his threatened attack. Later, when Nabal dies suddenly, David woos Abigail, and she becomes his second wife.

The name *Nabal* means "foolish" or "senseless," and suggests something of the character of its owner. Nabal is to be contrasted with Abigail who is intelligent, charming, and beautiful. She is a perfect match for David who possesses the same qualities.

Abigail's two speeches not only calm David's injured pride, they also divert him from committing a serious breach of divine law, namely bloodguilt. Instead of relying on the Lord, David was about to act on his own initiative. This is precisely Saul's flaw. But Abigail intercedes, and David is rescued from yet another danger. Again, the Lord is carefully directing the affairs of David so that he becomes a king without blemish, wholly obedient to God's will.

1 Samuel 26—David Spares Saul's Life

Returning to the conflict between David and Saul, we read a second account of how David spares Saul's life. (See also Chapter 24.) While the details differ, the message of both versions is the same. David, as the Lord's anointed servant, exercises righteousness and good faith toward Saul.

David's refusal to allow the murder of Saul is important in his rise to the throne. David has God's providential guidance. His history is God's history. Because David allows the Lord to direct his affairs, he is blessed and revered among all Israel's kings.

DIMENSION THREE:
WHAT DOES THE BIBLE MEAN TO ME?

1 Samuel 21:1-6—Human Needs Versus Institutions

When David takes the consecrated bread from Ahimelech, he makes a bold assertion. Since this bread is customarily reserved for the priest or for duly consecrated persons, David places the physical needs of his troops over religious regulation. When Jesus collects grain on the sabbath and heals on the sabbath, he also places human needs over cultic practices. In fact, Jesus even refers to David's actions. Observance of dietary regulations and holy days are important forms of service to the Lord. But sometimes other obligations must take priority. Both Jesus and David recognized these occasions and acted accordingly.

Regular participation in the fellowship of the church—including contributions of time, talent, and money—is important in the practice of Christian faith. However, there are times and circumstances when human need must prevail over the institutional requirements of the church. These needs may be personal, family, business, or physical needs. Each person must decide what these needs are and how they are to be met. What needs do you have that supercede the needs of the church? How can we decide which of our needs fall into this category?

1 Samuel 25:23-35—Divine Leadership

Had it not been for Abigail, David would have failed to submit to God's leadership. This is one of the most difficult lessons for Christians to learn. Most of us affirm and practice self-reliance, drawing our strength from ourselves. But the will of the Lord is an energy reserve we can tap into through faith. And the life of faith in turn affects all our actions.

The precise meaning of submitting to God's leadership will vary from person to person, and from place to place. God does not expect all of us to do the same thing. At the center of each response is the belief that this is God's will for me. That belief is crucial. In what areas of your life do you see God's leadership?

*Saul took his own sword
and fell on it (31:4).*

—— 7 ——
Saul's Last Days
1 Samuel 27–31

DIMENSION ONE:
WHAT DOES THE BIBLE SAY?

Answer these questions by reading 1 Samuel 27

1. To what city does David flee? Who is king? (27:2)

2. What does Saul do when he hears of David's defection to the Philistines? (27:4)

3. How long does David stay with the Philistines? (27:7)

4. How does David gain the confidence of Achish? (27:8-12)

Answer these questions by reading 1 Samuel 28

5. What position in his army does Achish give David? (28:2)

6. Who does Saul expel from Israel? (28:3)

7. Who does Saul visit for help? (28:7-8)

8. With whom does Saul wish to speak? (28:11)

9. What does Samuel tell Saul? (28:16-19)

10. What else does the medium do? (28:24-25)

Answer these questions by reading 1 Samuel 29

11. Why don't the Philistines want David to fight with them? (29:4)

12. What is Achish's response to their objections? (29:9-10)

Answer these questions by reading 1 Samuel 30

13. What do David and his men discover when they return to Ziklag? (30:3)

14. What does David do? (30:6-9)

15. How does David find the Amalekites? (30:13-15)

16. How does David distribute the booty taken from the Amalekites? (30:21-31)

Answer these questions by reading 1 Samuel 31

17. How does Saul die? (31:4)

18. Who else dies in battle that day? (31:2)

19. What do the Philistines do when they discover Saul's body? (31:9-10)

20. Who removes Saul's body and gives it a proper burial? (31:11-13)

DIMENSION TWO:
WHAT DOES THE BIBLE MEAN?

1 Samuel 27:1–28:2—
David in the Service of the Philistines

Saul's unrelenting pursuit drives David to seek shelter with Achish, king of the Philistine city of Gath. In return for military service, Achish awards David Ziklag, a city in Judah between Beersheba and Gath. From Ziklag, David stages raids against enemies such as the Geshurites, the Girzites, and the Amalekites. Yet, he assures Achish that his raids are against Judah's cities. This period of service lasts for one year and four months.

One of the remarkable features of the Old Testament is its profound honesty. Nowhere is this honesty more evident than in the stories of David. In David's defection to the Philistines, we see Israel's future king—God's own anointed leader—selling his military services to Israel's principal enemy. Although he never once lifts a hand against his own people, the very idea that David collaborates with the enemy is treasonous. In the stories of the slaughter at Nob (Chapter 21), and his adulterous crimes in his affair with Bathsheba, David is a genuinely fallible human being with shortcomings and weaknesses. Perhaps this curious combination of saint and sinner is what makes Old Testament characters real.

David's enlistment in Achish's service seems a roundabout way to the throne. But two points must be remembered. First, David never attacked or injured his own people. His cunning was sufficient to permit him to impress Achish without ruining his reputation or offending God. Second, David has an opportunity to enrich other cities of Judah because of his victory over the Amalekite raiders of Ziklag. Thus, while his year of foreign service is by no means laudatory, it does not impede his loyal service to God. With Saul's death near, David continues to strengthen his powerful position in Judah. He is destined to emerge as the ruler not only of southern Israel but also of Saul's domain in the North.

1 Samuel 28:3-25—Saul Consults the Medium at Endor

The account of Saul's conversation with the medium at Endor shows Saul's desperation. Earlier, Saul banned mediums and spiritists from practicing in Israel. Facing a serious Philistine threat at Gilboa, Saul tries in vain to contact the Lord. At last, he turns to a medium and tries to communicate with the dead.

A sleepy and ghost-like Samuel is conjured up by the medium, and his cheerless news to Saul mirrors his feelings about being disturbed. Because of Saul's remorse at Samuel's foreboding message he does not want to eat. Only through the coaxing of his servants and the medium does Saul finally regain his composure and appetite. With no further reprieves, Saul leaves to meet the destiny Samuel forecast for him.

One of the important contrasts between the early religion of Israel and that of her neighbors is her rejection of mediums and spiritists. Laws that prohibit consorting with mediums and spiritists are recorded in Leviticus 19:31 and 20:6. Saul expelled them from Israel. That he violated his own ban is an indication of his despair. The shame and disgrace of his consulting a medium is dramatized by the fact that it occurred at night. The entire mood of the encounter is sinister.

The list of customary modes of revelation in Israel found in verse 6 includes dreams and the sacred lots (Urim and Thummim). The final form of divine communication is through God's prophets. All these channels are now closed to Saul. He is totally alone, without the Lord.

He asks the medium to "bring up Samuel." He wants her to bring Samuel up from Sheol, or the realm of the dead beneath the earth. When an Israelite died, body and soul together went to Sheol, a dark, damp, dreary place. In Sheol people sleep and maintain little or no social contact. Sheol's inhabitants are ghost-like and eerie. Although Sheol is within God's reach, it is devoid of God's blessings.

Samuel's news to Saul is shocking. Tomorrow Saul faces death. His career as Israel's first king is drawing to a rapid conclusion. Completely separated from the Lord, haunted by evil spirits, and consumed by jealousy for David, Saul now must bear the ultimate consequence for his disobedience. The news causes Saul to go into a stupor. When he finally regains touch with reality, he eats and leaves. Saul goes forth to face the enemy, knowing that this is his final battle.

1 Samuel 29—David Is Rejected by the Philistines

In this brief chapter, David is spared choosing between disloyalty to Achish and fighting against his own people. The conflict is resolved when the Philistine commanders refuse to allow David to participate in the battle against Saul. Although David has the confidence of King Achish, the suspicions of the Philistine commanders probably would have proven correct.

The phrase "fight against the enemies of my lord the king" is ambiguous. Is David referring to Achish or Saul? Most commentators think David would have used the opportunity to turn on the Philistines in order to prove his loyalty to Saul and the men of Israel.

With the mention of the Philistine assembly at Aphek, we encounter a geographical problem. Earlier in 28:4, it is reported that they have encamped at Shunem, forty-five miles north of Aphek. Perhaps they were at Aphek, preparing to march to Shunem. Somehow they managed to move northward, since in 31:1 they are at Mount Gilboa.

Only foreigners, when referring to Israelites, would call them "Hebrews" (verse 3). David obviously lacks the confidence with these other leaders that characterizes his relationship with Achish. The commanders even cite the song sung earlier about David's exploits (18:7). They argue that it would be impossible for David to justify his treason to Saul or any of his countrymen. Thus, David is released by Achish, and he returns to Ziklag. David seems to be protected by the Lord.

1 Samuel 30—David and the Amalekites

This narrative recounts David's retaliation against an Amalekite raiding party that destroyed Ziklag. The story of the Philistine assault against Saul is temporarily sidetracked. As the story goes, while David is at Aphek with Achish (Chapter 29),

SAUL'S LAST DAYS

59

Israel's age-old enemies, the Amalekites, use the opportunity to raid Ziklag. The city is burned, and all its inhabitants are taken captive.

When David and his troops return, they weep at the devastation. Threats of mutiny arise. David consults the ephod to determine the Lord's will. He begins immediate pursuit, assured by the Lord of victory. They find an ill Egyptian slave abandoned by the Amalekites. After being fed, the slave leads David and his troops to the Amalekites who are leisurely enjoying their sports.

David attacks the city, frees the captives, and regains their stolen possessions from Ziklag, along with some animals of the Amalekites. David generously divides the booty among all his soldiers, including some men who were unable to participate in the final assault. David also distributes some of the wealth to rulers of small Judean cities as a gesture of his real loyalty.

This story helps explain David's great popularity in Judah. Not only is he an able military leader, but he is also a generous and fair-minded ruler. When Saul dies, David is the natural choice as successor. Also, this story contrasts the success of David with the failure of Saul. Although things seem bleak at first when David returns to find Ziklag ablaze, he is able to turn tragedy into triumph with the help of the Lord. Saul, on the other hand, finds no help at all.

1 Samuel 31—The Death of Saul

The scene for this chapter shifts northward again to Mount Gilboa and the valley of Jezreel. Saul and his troops fight the Philistines, and it does not go well for the Israelites. Saul's sons Jonathan, Abinadab, and Malki-Shua are slain, and Saul is badly wounded. Fearing torture or ridicule if discovered, Saul pleads with his armor-bearer to kill him. But his armor-bearer refuses. So Saul takes his own sword and ends his life.

The words of Samuel (28:19) come true. Saul and his sons are dead. But the throne has not yet passed on to David. Saul's reign has been characterized by a mixture of success and failure, of obedience and disobedience, of blessing and judgment. Saul made the first attempt at uniting the Israelite tribes, at least in terms of establishing a standing army. Also, he slowed the Philistine advance and managed to keep some cities in Israelite hands. But he was also a person beset by envy and paranoia. His disobedience transformed the Lord into his adversary.

DIMENSION THREE: WHAT DOES THE BIBLE MEAN TO ME?

1 Samuel 28:3-25—The Nature of Revelation

One of the central theological issues that arises from these chapters is the nature of revelation. When he saw the large size and potential danger of the Philistine army, Saul panicked. He was frantic with fear! So he chose to inquire of the Lord (28:6) in order to acquire courage and guidance. But his requests were to no avail! None of the usual channels of communication were open to him—neither the dreams, nor the Urim-Thummim, nor the prophets. The Lord refused to talk with Saul because of the king's sin. Even Samuel, who is summoned from Sheol by a medium, tells Saul that God has turned away from him. Saul is now totally alone. There is no revelation for him.

While to us the ancient modes of revelation available to Saul may seem suspect, early Israel found them to be a source of divine knowledge. The Lord often spoke through dreams. (See Genesis 28:10-22 and 37:5-11.) Our modern understanding speaks of dreams as unconscious desires or momentary preoccupations. What conflict do you see between the biblical view of dreams and our modern, psychological interpretation?

Few persons today would be willing to trust the sacred lots—if we had them—to give the divine word. Yet throughout the period of Samuel, Saul, and David, these small objects provided clear and trustworthy information. In the hands of the proper persons the Urim and Thummim were potent. As with dreams, we may have reservations about the use of such a device today.

SAUL'S LAST DAYS **61**

The third type of revelation Saul sought was the prophet. We too believe that God chooses certain persons as the recipients of special words. Who are the prophets of today? What are the signs or indications of their authority?

In discussing and evaluating biblical forms of revelation, we must be conscious that both the media and the message may change. The Lord addressed specific persons in specific situations. Both the persons and the situations are now different. We do God a disservice by limiting the deity to historical forms of revelation. The Bible provides an authoritative witness to God's work among the chosen people. But in the variety of types of revelations, the Bible also unlocks the door for God to address us in different ways. How can we remain open and sensitive to the Lord's word?

Then the men of Judah . . . anointed David king
over the house of Judah (2:4).

— 8 —

David the King

2 Samuel 1–4

DIMENSION ONE:
WHAT DOES THE BIBLE SAY?

Answer these questions by reading 2 Samuel 1

1. What news does the man from Saul's camp bring David at Ziklag? (1:4)

2. What proof does this man have that Saul is dead? (1:10)

3. How do David and his men react to the news of Saul's death? (1:11-12)

4. Why does David punish the man who brought him the news? (1:16)

5. Where is David's lament over Saul and Jonathan recorded? (1:18)

Answer these questions by reading 2 Samuel 2

6. Following Saul's death, where does the Lord tell David to go? (2:1)

7. Which office do the men of Judah award David when he arrives at Hebron? (2:4)

8. Who is named king of Israel to succeed Saul? (2:8-9)

9. How long does David reign as king of Judah at Hebron? (2:11)

10. Who are the two leaders of the conflict between Ish-Bosheth and David? (2:12-13)

11. Who wins the initial battle? (2:17)

12. Which relative of Joab does Abner slay? (2:23)

Answer these questions by reading 2 Samuel 3

13. Which sons of David were born at Hebron? (3:2-5)

14. How does Ish-Bosheth make Abner angry? (3:7-8)

15. What offer does Abner make to David? (3:21)

16. What does Joab do to Abner? (3:27)

17. What is David's response to the killing of Abner? (3:28-29)

Answer these questions by reading 2 Samuel 4

18. What is the relationship between Jonathan and Mephi-bosheth? (4:4)

19. What do the sons of Rimmon, Recab and Baanah, do to Ish-Bosheth? (4:7-8)

20. How does David respond to their deed? (4:12)

DIMENSION TWO:
WHAT DOES THE BIBLE MEAN?

2 Samuel 1—Saul and Jonathan Die

In the first half of this chapter, David learns of the deaths of Saul and Jonathan. An anonymous Amalekite appears in David's camp with the sad news. When David interrogates him, he confesses to killing the king who had already been fatally wounded. David instantly sentences the man to death. Not even Saul's crown and armlet assuages David's anger toward the Amalekite. David then instigates a period of mourning and fasting for the two fallen heroes.

We have already read one report of Saul's death in 1 Samuel 31. The earlier account reports that Saul takes his own life, whereas in the Amalekite's version he kills Saul to ease his suffering. Perhaps the Amalekite invented his version in hopes of winning David's favor. Obviously, his plot backfired.

As part of his public expression of grief over Saul and Jonathan, David composes a moving and eloquent song (verses 19-27). This type of eulogy or lament was sung in ancient Israel to honor the passing of national leaders. The beauty and incisiveness of these songs reside in their capacity to touch basic emotions and wake genuine pathos at the tragedy at hand. Certainly, David's lament for Saul and Jonathan qualifies as one of the finest songs in the Old Testament.

The Bible spares no detail to insure our understanding that David's grief is genuine. The deaths of Saul and Jonathan affect him profoundly. Despite Saul's frantic efforts to kill him, David is sincerely sad at his passing. The covenant of brotherhood between David and Jonathan is one of the truly deep relationships in the Old Testament, and the loss of this relationship is a source of grief. The Amalekite is wrong; David does not rejoice in anticipation of succeeding Saul. Instead he cries remorsefully,
"Your glory, O Israel, lies slain on your heights.
How the mighty have fallen!"

2 Samuel 2:1-11— David Becomes King Over Judah

With Saul dead, David assumes political leadership in Judah. But first he consults the Lord to determine God's will. Once the Lord approves, then David and his men proceed to Hebron where he is anointed king. One of his first acts as king is to praise the men of Jabesh Gilead for their kindness toward Saul. This act solidifies his claim to the Northern Kingdom. The next section (verses 8-11) relates the crowning of Ish-Bosheth, Saul's son, as king over Israel.

Chapter 2 illustrates well the theological view of history in the Bible. A modern historian would have been interested in following up on the details of the Philistine victory at Mount Gilboa. How much of the north now lies in their hands? Why do they allow David to be crowned king in the south? Instead, the Bible focuses our attention on the Lord's approval of David's enthronement. Because the Bible is interested in the theological dimension, we find it difficult to reconstruct a historically accurate record of events.

Abner's appointment of Ish-Bosheth as king over Israel delays David's kingship over the north for seven years. The name *Ish-Bosheth* was formerly *Esh-Baal* (1 Chronicles 8:33; 9:39). The word *baal* generally means "lord," but is also the name of a Canaanite god. Later biblical writers thought it improper to have the son of a famous Israelite leader named after a rival god.

The number *forty,* ascribed to Ish-Bosheth's age when he assumed power, is doubtful. Most commentators feel that Ish-Bosheth was quite young, perhaps even a boy, when Saul died. When Abner dies, Ish-Bosheth's rule collapses.

2 Samuel 2:12–3:39—Judah's War Against Israel

Soon after the accessions of David and Ish-Bosheth to the thrones of Judah and Israel, civil war breaks out between them. Two of the major antagonists in this conflict are Abner, Ish-Bosheth's commander, and Joab, David's commander. Tensions increase when Abner kills Asahel, Joab's brother. (See 2:23.)

Things go badly for Israel, while Judah grows strong. To make matters worse, Ish-Bosheth accuses Abner of disloyalty to his father when Abner seduces one of Saul's concubines. Abner then suggests that David transfer leadership of Israel to him. David and Abner meet to discuss terms. When Joab learns of this conference, he is infuriated with David for trusting Abner. Still harboring hatred for Abner, Joab slays him in revenge (3:27).

To disassociate himself from Joab and his vengeful behavior, David condemns his commander and institutes a period of national mourning and fasting. Once again, David makes every possible effort to remain above reproach in his march toward the throne. Just as he laments the deaths of Saul and Jonathan, he grieves publicly for the slaying of Abner. No one can accuse David of conspiracy. His hands are clean.

Second Samuel 3:1 is a summary of events that must have taken place over several years. We may be certain that many hard battles occur during these years, and both small countries suffer greatly.

Ish-Bosheth's charge against Abner in 3:7 is a legal one. Customarily, a ruler's wives and concubines pass on to his successor. But it is an indication of Abner's real power that he takes Rizpah. After all, Abner himself says he is the real reason Ish-Bosheth has a kingdom in the first place. He angrily dismisses the charge as petty in relation to his contributions to Ish-Bosheth.

David's request for the return of Michal, his first wife, has political overtones. You may recall that when David fled Gibeah to escape Saul, the king took Michal and gave her to Paltiel. David is now reclaiming his wife, thereby strengthening his claim as legitimate heir to the throne of Israel.

Joab's brutal and vengeful slaying of Abner is truly one of the low points in David's history. Usually, David punishes such actions by death, as in the case of the opportunistic Amalekite (1:15) and Ish-Bosheth's assassins (4:12). But Joab is kin (his nephew) and also a powerful military leader. Death is out of the question. So David places a curse against Joab and his family (3:29). This curse, along with David's public lament and mourning, clearly underscore David's innocence in the whole sordid affair.

2 Samuel 4—The Death of Ish-Bosheth

The event that finally opens the door for David's accession to the throne of Israel is the brutal murder of Ish-Bosheth. The perpetrators of this act are two members of the king's raiding party, Baanah and Recab. Thinking that they have done David a great favor, they revel before him in their deed. But David takes no joy in their debauchery. Instead, he punishes them by taking their lives. He clearly wishes to become king over Israel, but not by murder.

David is now on the verge of fulfilling his divine mandate to rule over all Israel, as the people of God. All barriers are gone; all detours have been eliminated. In the next lesson, David becomes king over the northern tribes as well as the southern tribes.

DIMENSION THREE:
WHAT DOES THE BIBLE MEAN TO ME?

2 Samuel 3:26-30—Motives for Punishment

Joab and Abishai take punitive action against Abner (3:30) for his slaying of Asahel their brother. Their actions are motivated entirely by revenge. Murder is punishable by murder. While the Old Testament is clear that ultimate vengeance belongs to God, the prevailing custom among the early tribes clearly called for blood vengeance. In the New Testament, Jesus counsels meeting hostility with love (Matthew 5:38-41). In our criminal justice system there is considerable disagreement over what should be the principal intent behind our laws and sentencing procedures. How should we respond to anti-social behavior? How can we love the lawbreaker?

2 Samuel 3:31-39—The Limitations of Leadership

The second issue in today's lesson is the limitation of leaders to function effectively and ethically. David finds himself unable to manage an aggressive and vengeful staff. Joab and Abishai are too much for him to handle. He realizes their actions are wrong, but he lacks the resources to discipline them. They are too powerful to be treated as ordinary citizens. So David admits his limitations and leaves their case in the hands of the Lord. Do you think this action shows a weakness in the king's character? Why or why not?

In American history there have been many incidents where top political leaders have been embarrassed by the behavior of their staff members. Presidential leadership has been jeopardized by the improper behavior of their cabinets and other advisors. But leaders must maintain accountability. They must select their top aides wisely.

As citizens we must be wary of imposing a double standard of morality on elected officials. Why must their hands be cleaner than our hands? How should David be blamed for Joab's revenge? How was David's potential service to the people of God lessened by Joab's aggressiveness? How did Joab's behavior reflect on David? How do the actions of our political leaders reflect on us?

All the elders of Israel ... . anointed David
king over Israel (5:3).

—— 9 ——
The Empire of David
2 Samuel 5–8

DIMENSION ONE:
WHAT DOES THE BIBLE SAY?

Answer these questions by reading 2 Samuel 5

1. What responsibility do the elders of Israel bestow upon David? (5:3)

2. How long does David rule over Israel and Judah together? (5:5)

3. Who occupies Jerusalem at David's inauguration? (5:6)

4. How does David infiltrate Jerusalem and overcome the Jebusites? (5:8)

5. Which neighboring king sends men and materials to David for the construction of a royal palace? (5:11)

6. What traditional enemy attacks Israel after David becomes king? (5:17)

Answer these questions by reading 2 Samuel 6

7. What sacred object does David wish to bring into Jerusalem? (6:2)

8. Why does Uzzah die during the march to Jerusalem? (6:6-7)

9. How does David react to Uzzah's death? (6:8-10)

10. What does David do as the ark enters Jerusalem? (6:14)

11. How does Michal, David's wife, react to David's behavior? (6:16)

Answer these questions by reading 2 Samuel 7

12. Who is Nathan? (7:2)

13. What does David say to Nathan? (7:2)

14. What does the Lord promise David? (7:10)

15. Who does the Lord say will build God's house? (7:12-13)

Answer these questions by reading 2 Samuel 8

16. Who does David conquer during his reign over Israel and Judah? (8:11-12)

17. Who is the recorder during David's tenure as king? (8:16)

18. Who are David's priests? (8:17)

19. Who is the royal secretary? (8:17)

DIMENSION TWO:
WHAT DOES THE BIBLE MEAN?

2 Samuel 5—David, King of Israel and Judah

This chapter describes three incidents, all relating to David's accession to the throne. First, David becomes king over the northern tribes (5:1-5). Following Ish-Bosheth's death, the elders of Israel visit David at Hebron. There, he concludes a treaty with them whereby he becomes their king. The elders are the senior members of the ten tribes of the north. Actually, David is their only alternative, and, in truth, the rightful heir to Saul's throne. He has earned it by virtue of his marriage to Saul's daughter, by his excellent service in Saul's army, and by the Lord's promise.

The second incident is David's conquest of Jerusalem (5:6-16). Jerusalem is the one city that remained unconquered by the invading Hebrews under Joshua. It is inhabited by the Jebusites who are distant relatives of the Canaanites. Jerusalem is also a very good place for a capital. Neither the north nor the south could take offense at such a central location as Jerusalem. Also, Jerusalem is an excellent site as David's citadel because it is one of the higher points in the immediate region, bounded by valleys on three sides.

One of David's greatest accomplishments in Israelite history is the final resolution of the Philistine menace. In verses 17-25, this warfare is described briefly. Doubtless, it required several years for David to complete this task. Notice that David consults the Lord before instituting warfare. The Lord rewards David's propriety with victory.

2 Samuel 6—David and the Ark

David and his men make an initial effort to transport the ark into Jerusalem, his new capital. All goes well until suddenly, the oxen pulling the cart stumble and Uzzah is struck dead when he tries to prevent the ark from falling. After three months, a second attempt is made, and this time it is successful. David leaps and dances in celebration of the arrival of the sacred object. But Michal, his wife, chides him for such a public display. David responds by permanently estranging her.

Verse 1 tells us that David gathered 30,000 men to bring the ark to Jerusalem. This number is unusually high. Certainly, an important occasion such as this demands proper escort, but we cannot be certain why so many men are brought. The last mention of the ark in 1 Samuel 7:2 has Kiriath Jearim as its resting place. How does it get from there to Baalah of Judah?

Some commentators believe that these are two different names for the same place.

The wrath of the Lord against the unfortunate Uzzah frightens David, and gives him cause to temporarily abandon his mission. The Hebrew of this passage makes it difficult to envision the series of events leading to Uzzah's death. Regardless of where he stood in relation to the sacred object, Uzzah violates the sanctity of the Lord and pays with his life. God's holiness must be respected.

Even David wonders now about his fitness to transport the ark (verse 9). So for three months, while the Lord's anger abates, the ark rests at the home of Obed-Edom. The blessing of Obed-Edom is the sign that a proper interval has elapsed and God is no longer angry. Now David completes his mission and the ark enters Jerusalem.

The story of Michal's anger explains her barrenness that ends Saul's dynasty forever. Michal pays a high price for her harsh words to David. Exactly why Michal is angry with David is unclear. She may have been upset at being snatched from Paltiel. (See 2 Samuel 3:15-16.) She may not have enjoyed being a member of an ever-increasing harem. Or, she may have opposed the bringing in the ark for theological reasons. For whatever reason, her remarks evoke David's ire, and Saul's line is ended permanently.

2 Samuel 7—God's Covenant With David

Wishing to build a more ornate structure for the ark, David consults Nathan the prophet. Nathan tells David that the Lord does not desire a house, (that is, a dynasty). David then acknowledges God's special blessings given to him and offers appropriate words of thanksgiving.

Certainly, this chapter ranks among the most important in all the Old Testament. Here we have a divine legitimization of monarchy and a promise of its continuance. With the ark now in Jerusalem, the older Mosaic religion is now combined with the new idea of a monarchy. Kingship now has a political as well as a religious basis.

THE EMPIRE OF DAVID **75**

Nathan is David's official court prophet. He is a staff member of the royal court. Yet, he manages to retain his integrity and offers both support (7:3) and judgment (12:7). His presence in David's court cemented the relationship between church and state.

The terms of David's covenant are threefold: (1) to make David's name great, (2) to secure Israel in her land, and (3) to establish David's dynasty. This last point is the basis for royal succession in the south during the duration of her statehood. It is also the basis for associating the leadership of the people of God with a descendant of the house of David. Remember that Luke traces Jesus' ancestry back to David.

David's prayer (verses 18-29) is a model of piety and thanksgiving. He recounts the Lord's mighty deeds for Israel, and he pledges his loyalty and service to the Lord. In form and substance, it is a typical song of thanksgiving.

2 Samuel 8—David's Military Conquests

This chapter summarizes David's conquests of nearby nations and describes his administrative staff in Jerusalem. Most of these small kingdoms border Israel and were rivals for the control of the general region of Palestine. With these victories, David transforms Israel into a large state, extending from Dan in the north to Beersheba in the south. Israel now includes most of the nations to the east of the Jordan River, and southward to Edom. Under the leadership of David and Solomon, Israel attended the zenith of her political influence and military strength.

The list of officials in David's court confirms that a sizable bureaucracy is in the making. The small government of Saul rapidly gave way to the larger, more complex organization of David. David is in full control not only of Israel and Judah, but of much of the surrounding country as well. He has chosen a new capital, initiated a bureaucracy, and set government into motion. Most important, kingship and the Davidic dynasty have received the imprimatur of the Lord. The people of God have a leader.

DIMENSION THREE:
WHAT DOES THE BIBLE MEAN TO ME?

2 Samuel 6:1-15—Institutionalized Religion

David's decision to move the ark into Jerusalem is important for religious, military, social, and economic reasons. This move also carries the blessing of the Lord. But when David wants to build a temple to house the ark, the Lord stops him. God has not asked for a house.

The Lord cautions David with good reason. The portable ark represents God's close, dynamic interaction with the people. Where they go, the ark (and God) goes also. Everyone can see the holy object and rejoice in its powerful presence. To enshrine the ark in a building would surely lessen the intimacy between God and the people. Religion would become a conventional social institution rather than a moving force in persons' lives. To avoid this danger of institutionalizing religion, the Lord refuses to allow David to build a temple.

How does our religion suffer from excessive institutionalizing? Perhaps for some persons, the beautiful sanctuaries, high steeples, and stained glass windows fail to kindle a spark of religious fervor. Perhaps some sermons or church school lessons deal with peripheral issues and leave our souls thirsty for drink. Perhaps our participation in weekly services springs from motives other than our love for God.

On the other hand, many other persons find meaning and power through weekly proclamation of God's word. They rejoice in the fellowship and supportive ministries of the church. Consider all the social causes aided by church support: hospitals, nursing homes, orphanages, and meals-on-wheels. Perhaps the church lacks influence and authority for some persons. But for many others, it provides access to God's grace. What can we do to put life into our religious experiences? How can we let the church become our servant rather than our master?

THE EMPIRE OF DAVID

77

2 Samuel 7:18-29—David, Model of Faith

As a model of faith, David exhibits confidence, submission, and courage. These elements provide important clues to God's expectation of us.

David courageously seeks the Lord's counsel in moments of need and crisis. Certainty and clarity in understanding God's will leads to confident action. Second, like David we must learn to allow God to take the lead and to submit to God's guidance. We may practice submission in our personal value systems, in the use of our time, and in our relationships with other persons. God's will for our lives becomes clearer through inward spiritual growth. And finally, faith means courage. David's confidence and obedient submission would have accomplished little without the courage to act on his commitments. Like David, we can learn to manage our fears and not be disabled by them. David provides an excellent model of faith. How can we appropriate this model?

But the thing David had done
*displeased the L*ORD *(11:27).*

— 10 —
David, Bathsheba, and Solomon
2 Samuel 9–12

DIMENSION ONE:
WHAT DOES THE BIBLE SAY?

Answer these questions by reading 2 Samuel 9

1. Who is the servant of Saul that David locates? (9:2)

2. How does Ziba help David? (9:3)

3. What does David do for Mephibosheth? (9:7)

4. Who is Mica? (9:12)

Answer these questions by reading 2 Samuel 10

5. Why does David send his servants to Hanun, king of the Ammonites? (10:1-2)

6. How does Hanun treat David's servants? (10:4)

7. What do the Ammonites do next? (10:6)

8. What is the outcome of the battle? (10:13-14)

9. What does Hadadezer do after the first battle? (10:16)

Answer these questions by reading 2 Samuel 11

10. Who is Israel fighting at this time? (11:1)

11. Who is Bathsheba? (11:3-4)

12. Why does David's plan to conceal his affair fail? (11:9)

13. How does David arrange for Uriah to die? (11:15)

14. Following Uriah's death, what arrangements does David make for Bathsheba? (11:27)

15. What is the Lord's attitude toward the matter? (11:27)

Answer these questions by reading 2 Samuel 12

16. Who delivers the Lord's message to David? (12:1)

17. How does Nathan illustrate David's sin? (12:1-5)

18. How does the Lord punish David? (12:7-18)

19. What do David and Bathsheba name their second son? (12:24)

20. How does David treat the conquered Ammonites? (12:31)

DIMENSION TWO: WHAT DOES THE BIBLE MEAN?

2 Samuel 9—David Is Gracious to Mephibosheth

Recalling his covenant of friendship with Jonathan (1 Samuel 20:12-17), David asks if any of Saul's family is still alive. Through Ziba, a servant of Saul, David learns that a son of Jonathan survives whose name is Mephibosheth. Mephibosheth is quickly brought into David's court and welcomed with open arms by the king.

DAVID, BATHSHEBA, AND SOLOMON   **81**

The bond of friendship between Jonathan and David was one of the genuinely firm covenants in the Old Testament. The Bible shows that David's intentions in befriending Mephibosheth were not politically motivated. David's kindness is out of love for Jonathan.

The expression "dead dog" in 9:8 is a common derogatory term. Mephibosheth feels unworthy of David's great generosity. David's initial greeting, "Don't be afraid," allays Mephibosheth's suspicions that David's intentions are sinister. Such a fear is well founded, for in the ancient Near East new kings killed the families of the displaced ruler to avoid future claims to the throne. However, David restores family lands, servants, and personal dignity to Mephibosheth.

2 Samuel 10:1–11:1; 12:26-31—
David Defeats the Ammonites and the Arameans

This section summarizes David's military engagements against two hostile kingdoms east of the Jordan River. Few details of these battles are given. They serve mainly as a setting for David's affair with Bathsheba. Despite all David's military and political victories, he is still very human.

The conflict with the Ammonite/Aramean coalition begins by the intentional humiliation by Hanun of David's royal messengers. Nahash, Hanun's father (10:1), has died. Evidently, David and the deceased king had made some type of agreement earlier, and David is now honoring the covenant. The terms of their covenant are unknown. Perhaps their common bond involved a mutual dislike for Saul. At any rate, the new king, Hanun, does not share his father's friendly regard for David, but instead views him with suspicion and mistrust. He publicly embarrasses David's servants by cutting their beards and exposing their genitals, and thereby insults the king. David's response is swift and certain: compassion to the embarrassed men and a declaration of war against Ammon.

Most of the small kingdoms mentioned in 10:6-8 are located east and northeast of the Jordan River. What Joab encounters is a major war against a sizable coalition. Nevertheless, the superior training of David's troops leads to a clear victory.

The Arameans quickly regroup and prepare for a second battle. David responds this time with the standing army of Israel and engages Shobach, the Aramean commander, in battle. David accompanies his troops on this second encounter with the Arameans and their king, Hadadezer (2 Samuel 8:3). The defeated people now become servants to David.

The third set of battles involves a renewed attack against Ammon and its capital, Rabbah. The account of this conflict begins in 11:1 and is concluded in 12:26-31. But unlike the campaign against the Arameans, David does not accompany the troops until the final assault on Rabbah. He chooses to remain in Jerusalem. Once Joab and the troops of Israel have successfully surrounded the Ammonites at Rabbah, David joins the battle. The captive Arameans become David's servants. Their manual labor doubtless enlarges the royal work force, and their national booty expands the royal coffers. Israel's power and prestige in the region is definitely on the upswing.

2 Samuel 11:2–12:25—David and Bathsheba

These two chapters comprise one of the most revealing episodes of the Scriptures. Few documents—religious, historical, or literary—can compare with this narration for candor and honesty. The narration of an adulterous affair of the king of Israel, compounded by his conspiracy to murder, is both surprising and disappointing. Witnessing the moral failure of such a great and noble man as David is saddening. Perhaps the lesson for us lies in his responses to the situation.

The setting of the story is superbly described—late in the afternoon, in the early spring, when many of the men were away at war. Atop his roof, overlooking the entire city, the king's eye catches a glimpse of the beautiful Bathsheba bathing. He brings her to his house where they engage in illicit lovemaking. She becomes pregnant.

To conceal his immoral actions, David hastily recalls Uriah, her husband, from battle and invites him to spend a few days relaxing at home. During periods of war, Israelite soldiers were to remain pure and undefiled (1 Samuel 21). Uriah's deep commitment to celibacy during holy war precludes such pleasures. Finally, in desperation, David arranges Uriah's death. David and Bathsheba wed following a brief mourning period. "But the thing David had done displeased the LORD."

Although Uriah is called the Hittite, the name *Uriah* is a Hebrew name. The Hittites were a major power in Asia Minor in ancient times. Many Hittites settled in Palestine and adopted the religion of Israel. Uriah's father was probably a Hittite, whereas his son fully embraced the Israelite religion.

Uriah's murder is cloaked with the apparel of normal warfare. Joab, who wisely asks no questions about David's instructions, places Uriah at the forefront of the battle. Soon Uriah falls, along with other men from David's army. David's hasty marriage to Bathsheba spares them public embarrassment.

In verse 27, we read how God feels. God is upset with David. The same laws of morality are binding on king and subject alike—no double standard here. David's humanity is evident in his sin. God's anointed king now faces judgment.

Nathan is David's official court prophet. He is the bearer of divine words—first of judgment, then of promise. The beautiful parable of the rich man and the poor man clearly illustrates the hideous nature of injustice. In pronouncing judgment against the rich man, David condemns himself. Nathan's haunting words drive home the point: "You are the man!" No one escapes the watchful eye of the Lord.

God punishes David by continued family problems. David himself suffers the humiliation of Absalom's public rape of his harem. Also, Bathsheba's child dies, despite David's earnest prayers. David's acknowledgment of his sins (12:13) prompts God's partial forgiveness, but David still must be punished because of the seriousness of the offense.

The child's death is the atonement for David's sin. David is zealous in his mourning for the ill child. He seems to be so carried away by his grief that his servants fear for his safety once the child dies. Much to their surprise, when David finally learns the truth, he pulls himself together, gives praise to the Lord, and begins to eat again. The child is gone, he reasons, and there is no rescuing him from Sheol.

The name *Solomon* comes from a Hebrew word *shalom,* meaning "peace, wholeness, or prosperity." It suggests God's renewed blessing of David's house.

DIMENSION THREE:
WHAT DOES THE BIBLE MEAN TO ME?

2 Samuel 11:1-13—Sin and Punishment

Most of us are familiar with the problem of so-called double standards—one set of values for us and another set for everyone else. Teenagers often accuse their parents of having a double standard on certain issues. Several events in past years have raised this question in connection with the use or abuse of presidential authority.

When David commits adultery with Bathsheba, and compounds his sin by having her husband killed, the Lord punishes the king, his accomplice, and the innocent child. Adultery is wrong, regardless of who does it. Murder is still murder. David and Bathsheba pay a high price for their conduct.

What are some contemporary examples of double-standard morality? Why are these double standards unfair? How can concerned Christians begin to correct these injustices?

2 Samuel 11:26-27—God and Human Weakness

As you study the Old and New Testaments, you will learn that many of the great characters of the Bible commit sins from time to time. What were the sins of Noah, of Abraham, of Jacob, and of Moses?

Sometimes God uses human vessels who are conspicuously imperfect to move the kingdom forward. But, the lesson for us is that in the last analysis God does not depend on persons. The ultimate responsibility for salvation lies not with us, but with God. What role does Christ's atonement play in this analysis of humankind before God? Does standing under grace make us perfect persons? Why or why not?

*So [Absalom] stole the hearts
of the men of Israel (15:6).*

11
Absalom's Rebellion
2 Samuel 13–16

DIMENSION ONE:
WHAT DOES THE BIBLE SAY?

Answer these questions by reading 2 Samuel 13

1. How is Tamar related to Absalom? (13:1)

2. How does Amnon feel about Tamar? (13:1-2)

3. What does Amnon do to Tamar? (13:14-18)

4. How does Absalom respond to Amnon's abuse of Tamar?
   (13:23, 28)

5. Where does Absalom seek refuge? (13:37)

Answer these questions by reading 2 Samuel 14

6. Who wants David to bring Absalom back to Jerusalem? (14:1-2)

7. How does Joab convince David to bring Absalom back? (14:1-20)

8. How does David treat Absalom when he returns to Jerusalem? (14:24, 28)

9. Why does Absalom set fire to Joab's barley field? (14:29-30)

Answer these questions by reading 2 Samuel 15

10. How does Absalom gain popularity among the men of Israel? (15:1-6)

11. How does Absalom plot to gain the throne? (15:7-10)

12. What does David do after hearing about Absalom's conspiracy? (15:14)

13. How does Ittai, the Gittite, show loyalty toward David? (15:21)

14. What sacred object does David leave behind? (15:25)

15. Who does David ask to become a spy? (15:32-34)

Answer these questions by reading 2 Samuel 16

16. What charge does Ziba bring against Mephibosheth? (16:3)

17. What does David do? (16:4)

18. Why does Shimei curse the fleeing king? (16:7-8)

19. What is David's reaction to Shimei's cursing? (16:10-11)

20. What advice does Ahithophel give Absalom? (16:21)

DIMENSION TWO:
WHAT DOES THE BIBLE MEAN?

2 Samuel 13—Amnon's Sin and Absalom's Revenge

Amnon shows his father's passion for beautiful women. Amnon yearns for the affections of his beautiful half-sister, Tamar. Despite her protests and suggestions of a more proper way, Amnon rapes her.

Amnon is the eldest son of David. His mother is Ahinoam (2 Samuel 3:2). Absalom and Tamar are the offsprings of Maacah. Marriages between kin are not uncommon during the early days of Israel. Abraham, for instance, marries Sarah, his half-sister (Genesis 20:12). Later, however, such arrangements are banned by law (Leviticus 18:9). Thus, the real problem is Amnon's haste and impropriety in dealing with Tamar, compounded by his subsequent rejection of her.

Amnon's request for special food, prepared in his presence by a virgin, seems to be a reasonable one for David grants his permission immediately. The special food may have been thought to have a medicinal power, or perhaps it was intended merely to humor the ill person.

Following the rape of Tamar, Amnon suddenly feels a strong revulsion for her. We haven't a clue as to the cause of this change in attitude. Nevertheless, Tamar leaves in disgrace and seeks shelter with Absalom. The phrase "Tamar lived in her brother Absalom's house, a desolate woman" indicates that, because of this tragic and wanton act, she is no longer desirable as a wife. So she leads a lonely, solitary life in the house of her kin.

The sheep-shearing festival is a major celebration in Israel (1 Samuel 25:4-8). David has little reason for suspicion. Amnon's attendance as the heir-apparent is both fitting and proper. Following the assassination of Amnon, the other crown princes flee in chaotic confusion. This leads to faulty reports, at first, that everyone was dead. Jonadab eagerly seizes the opportunity to correct the misinformation supplied to David and informs him that only Amnon is dead. The sorrowful king, now bereft of two sons, is left in mourning.

2 Samuel 14—Absalom Returns to Jerusalem

The entire episode of Absalom's return to Jerusalem is undergirded by concern over the unresolved problem of succession. With Amnon, the eldest, now dead, and Kileab either dead or gone (after 3:3, he is never mentioned again), Absalom would be the successor. But before he can even be considered, he must be allowed to return from Geshur. Hence, Joab devises a plan to effect his return.

Tekoa is a village six miles south of Bethlehem. The woman from there is called "wise" because she can use the proper words to achieve a desired end. Joab actually writes the script of her fictitious story, though. The story she tells the king is a personal one, and it raises a genuine legal dilemma. By law, bloodguilt must be avenged by taking the life of the murderer. However, tradition and custom favored preservation of the family name through survival of an heir. In resolving the dilemma, David passes judgment on his own exile of Absalom. The survival of the Davidic dynasty is being jeopardized by the continued banishment of Absalom.

In verses 12-14, the woman discloses the real reason she has come to David—to secure the return of Absalom. The nation, she says, fears that Absalom will die in a foreign land and Israel will again be without leadership.

David quickly perceives the hand of Joab in the matter, and issues orders for Absalom's prompt return. But, instead of forgiving the banished son and restoring him to the royal fold, David keeps him at a distance and refuses to see him for two years. This seems only to compound Absalom's insecurity about succession and causes him to hate his father.

The story is briefly interrupted to describe Absalom. The weight of his hair is likely exaggerated, but is an ancient symbol of strength and favor. He is pictured as a handsome young man who deserves the throne. This picture is somewhat blurred by his rashness in getting Joab's attention. Absalom is clearly a man of impulse. Already we can see he is impatient for David's crown.

2 Samuel 15:1-12—Absalom's Rebellion

During the four years following his return from exile in Geshur, Absalom carefully sows seeds of discontent. He sympathizes with persons who have legal difficulties to win popularity and indicates that matters would be different if he were king. He even obtains a chariot, horsemen, and bodyguards, all to dramatize his position as king-apparent. Then, under the pretense of fulfilling a vow to the Lord, Absalom goes to Hebron, accompanied by two hundred men, to begin the revolt. One of David's trusted counselors, Ahithophel, is summoned to participate in the rebellion.

The gate where Absalom stands is probably one of the entrances into Jerusalem. In ancient times, legal disputes were often brought before the elders at the gate. David's failure to establish an appropriate judiciary system seems to be a weakness Absalom exposes here.

Hebron is an appropriate choice for Absalom to institute a rebellion, since it was David's first capital and Absalom's birthplace. There may have been lingering resentments over David's moving the capital to Jerusalem. David's suspicions would not have been raised by Absalom's request to go to Hebron, since Hebron was a major religious center in the South.

The Bible gives us only the barest details of Absalom's move to Hebron. Ahithophel and the two hundred persons who accompany Absalom to Hebron are persons who will be useful in establishing a new government. Ahithophel is Bathsheba's grandfather and may still resent David's scandalous affair.

2 Samuel 15:13–16:14—David's Flight From Jerusalem

David's flight from Jerusalem is hasty and somewhat surprising. The reasons why David chooses to abandon Jerusalem so quickly are unclear. Perhaps he suspects treason from within. Perhaps he wishes to spare the city from being destroyed by a great battle. Among the troops he reviews, the Kerethites and Pelethites are Philistine mercenary soldiers who attached themselves to David, as are Ittai and his troops from Gath.

David gives Ittai and his men the opportunity to return and serve Absalom.

David has two reasons not to include the ark in his flight. First, he wishes to leave the matter entirely in God's hands, and leaving the ark places his case before God. Second, having a few spies in Absalom's camp is an advantage.

David goes down out of the city, across the Kidron Valley, and up the Mount of Olives. Had David fled southward to his homeland in Judah, he would have met Absalom. Northward, the people of Israel have already registered their dissatisfaction by carrying legal matters to Absalom. Also, those Israelites from the tribes of Benjamin still harbor resentment toward David for the fates of Saul, Ish-Bosheth, and Abner. Once he is beyond the Jordan, there is ample wilderness to hide in and friends to give him aid and shelter.

Calling Hushai "David's friend" (verse 37) indicates he had a formal office. Hushai is from the Arkite tribe that settled near Bethel. He is sent back to help the priests spy on Absalom and Ahithophel.

Ziba's charges against Mephibosheth are later challenged in 19:25-27, as a triumphant David reenters his royal city. Surely the lame prince is more intelligent than to assume he will be restored to the throne by Absalom. David acts hastily when he gives Ziba the property. Ziba's story about Mephibosheth's defection to Absalom is shaky. David's final resolution of the conflict is to divide the property and goods equally between Mephibosheth and Ziba. (See 19:25.)

The words of Shimei in 16:7-8 doubtless reflect the anger and frustration of many members of the house of Saul. To them, David is a usurper of Saul's throne and the murderer of his son and general. David protects Shimei, thinking that this charge is possibly part of his punishment.

The sad picture we see is of a mighty king fleeing from his beloved city in the wake of a rebellion led by his own son. Even the support he receives from trustworthy and loyal servants such as Ittai and Hushai cannot dim his grief. Not even the cursing of Shimei provokes the king's defensiveness. David shows his great faith by placing the entire matter before God for final arbitration.

2 Samuel 16:15-23—Absalom Assumes Power

No sooner has David left, than Absalom enters Jerusalem as king. "All the men of Israel" (verse 15) refers to the general army that accompanies Absalom. Hushai, David's spy, quickly gains Absalom's favor. Hushai's attachment to Absalom is met, wisely, by suspicion. Since Husshai held the respected position as the "king's friend," Absalom wonders how he can switch loyalties so quickly. Only through flattery does Hushai succeed. He claims Absalom's rule is by divine election and popular acclaim. Who could resist such words? Certainly not the vain and egocentric Absalom.

Ahithophel urges Absalom to complete his coup d'etat by publicly having sexual intercourse with the ten royal concubines David left behind. It was the custom for a new king to assert his rule and his power by taking over the concubines of the deposed ruler. The tent (2 Samuel 16:22) is perhaps similar to a wedding tent and still survives today in the form of the canopy used at Jewish weddings. The act shows that now Absalom is in charge.

DIMENSION THREE:
WHAT DOES THE BIBLE MEAN TO ME?

2 Samuel 15:24-29—David's Trust in the Lord

As David and his entourage leave Jerusalem, the priests bring along the sacred ark. But, much to their astonishment, David stops them, and tells them to return the ark to Jerusalem. In view of David's past reliance on the ark, and his frequent consultation of the divine will, it seems strange that he now separates himself from an important source of strength and guidance. His son is leading a rebellion and many of his supporters are defecting. If there is ever a time in his life when he needs divine confirmation, it is now that his kingdom is in jeopardy.

What does David's action tell us about his character? When have you demonstrated trust and courage in the Lord? In these situations, did you feel a sense of helplessness and despair? Why, or why not?

2 Samuel 16:15-23—Absalom's Trust in Human Counsel

Absalom's aggressive revolt provides a useful model of the person who relies solely on human wisdom. Absalom trusts human counsel whereas David trusts the Lord. Consequently, Absalom's revolt fails. Absalom never consults the Lord. He acts violently and deceptively toward other persons. He is motivated mainly by greed and lust for power.

Who else have we studied in these lessons that exhibited this prideful self-reliance? What happened to him? How can we achieve a balance between passively accepting God's will and having complete independence?

And for the whole army the victory that day was
turned into mourning (19:2).

—— 12 ——
David Regains
His Throne
2 Samuel 17–20

DIMENSION ONE:
WHAT DOES THE BIBLE SAY?

Answer these questions by reading 2 Samuel 17

1. How does Ahithophel tell Absalom to conquer David? (17:1-2)

2. Who else does Absalom consult? (17:5)

3. How does Hushai's advice differ from Ahithophel's? (17:11)

4. How does Hushai warn David? (17:17)

5. What does Ahithophel do when he learns that Absalom disregarded his advice? (17:23)

6. Who does Absalom choose to replace Joab as head of his army? (17:25)

7. Who befriends David during his stay at Mahanaim? (17:27)

Answer these questions by reading 2 Samuel 18

8. What does David tell Joab, Abishai, and Ittai as they go out to fight Absalom? (18:5)

9. What do Joab and his men do with Absalom when they find him in a tree? (18:14-15)

10. How do they bury Absalom? (18:17)

11. Who tells David of Absalom's death? (18:32)

Answer these questions by reading 2 Samuel 19

12. What does Joab tell David? (19:7-8)

13. Who does David appoint as commander of his army? (19:13)

14. How does King David treat Shimei? (19:23)

15. What does David do after Mephibosheth explains why he did not flee with the king? (19:29)

16. Who does the aged Barzillai send to go with the king? (19:37)

Answer these questions by reading 2 Samuel 20

17. Who leads a minor revolt against David? (20:2)

18. Who kills Amasa? (20:10)

19. How does Joab stop the revolt of Sheba without destroying Abel Beth Maacah where Sheba is staying? (20:16-22)

20. Who are the officials in David's government at this time? (20:23-26)

DIMENSION TWO:
WHAT DOES THE BIBLE MEAN?

2 Samuel 17—David Reaches Safety

Had Absalom followed Ahithophel's counsel and moved quickly to kill David, he could have strengthened his hold on the throne and eliminated his main resistance. His kingship would have been secure. Ahithophel's image of the bride coming to her husband suggests devotion and loyalty. That Ahithophel's counsel pleased Absalom suggests that the new king is completely without moral conscience. His ambition knows no limits.

But Absalom pauses to solicit a second option. This delay buys precious time for David to cross the Jordan, regroup his forces, and prepare a strategy for battle. Hushai's speech is masterful. His images are vivid. His eloquence is convincing and Absalom prefers his counsel. The speech also appeals to the vanity of the glory-seeking young king. The Lord again operates behind the scenes.

Evidently, once Hushai presents his plan, he retires to wait while the final decision is made. Meanwhile, he warns David of impending danger by way of a prearranged intelligence network. A maiden fetching water at a common well would arouse little suspicion. But the two informants are spotted and must think of a way to avoid discovery. They then escape to tell David to move quickly.

The account of Ahithophel's suicide is told calmly with no hint of scandal or disgrace. He chooses to end his life, not because his pride has been wounded, but because he realizes now that the young king's days are numbered. By delaying his attack, Absalom gives David time to prepare. Ahithophel knows this delay will be fatal, and David will show him no mercy.

Mahanaim is the site of the short-lived and feeble administration of Ish-Bosheth, Saul's son. Shobi probably is a brother or a close relative of the ungrateful Hanun (2 Samuel 10:1-5). Makir is the man who offered shelter to the lamed Mephibosheth (2 Samuel 9:4-5). Barzillai appears later as a wealthy patron of David who gives him Kimham (2 Samuel 19:37). This support in the region east of the Jordan shows that David's influence and prestige are far from exhausted. Now, David prepares for battle with his son. Absalom leaves him no choice but to fight.

2 Samuel 18—Absalom Dies

The structure of David's small but highly skilled army is appropriate for armies of that period. The units of thousands and hundreds designate rank or importance rather than precise numbers. Absalom's large but untrained army quickly falls apart under assault from David's men. The location of the "forest of Ephraim" is difficult to determine. The general region of Ephraim is located far to the west of the Jordan and twenty to thirty miles north of Jerusalem. Yet, there is no mention of David's troops crossing the river again. Perhaps the forest of Ephraim refers to a small region east of the Jordan, settled by near-relatives of the Palestinian Ephraimites of the central hill country.

Absalom's head gets caught in a tree. This, and the way Joab and his men kill him, further degrade the man and his cause. Despite David's orders to Joab to deal gently with Absalom, Joab mercilessly draws blood with darts, then his men finish the job. Absalom's body is tossed into a pit and covered with rocks.

Joab's initial refusal to let Ahimaaz deliver the news of Absalom's death to David reflects his knowledge that bad news is often met by an angry king (2 Samuel 1:16). Instead, an Ethiopian slave bears the message. Ahimaaz finally persuades Joab, takes a quicker route, and outruns the Cushite to David. But he is unable to tell the king his son is dead. David must await the other messenger and even then the message is unclear. David gets the point, and he is profuse in his grief. David's love for his son contrasts with Absalom's desire to depose his father. David's words of grief over Absalom have become a proverb of fatherly love (verse 33).

2 Samuel 19—David Returns to Jerusalem

Despite his impulsiveness and tendency toward violence, Joab has a keen sense of political propriety. He senses the feelings of rejection among David's supporters. The king is more upset over the death of a traitor than he is joyous over regaining his throne. *Would David be so distressed had he lost, but Absalom been spared?* they thought. Joab's threat of further rebellions moves David to acknowledge the rightful honors due his troops.

First David tries to unite a fractured kingdom by reaffirming his kinship with the south. He names Amasa, a former leader of Absalom's forces, as his chief commander. David's motives for the appointment are unclear. Perhaps David wishes to placate the southern tribesmen by including one of their own in his new army. On the other hand, maybe David intends to punish Joab for slaying Absalom.

The men of Judah waste no time in hastening to greet David as king. Meanwhile, the men of Israel are also slowly rallying to support the victorious king, in the absence of a more suitable candidate. This section (verses 8b-15) along with verses 41-43 suggest deep-seated divisions between the ten tribes of Israel and the two tribes of Judah. Here, it taxes even David to restore harmony to the rival tribes.

David again encounters Shimei, the cursing, dirt-throwing Benjamite. His apology meets with a word of forgiveness from David. The king's grace toward Shimei, however, is calculated only to restore harmony to the country. David later instructs Solomon to have him killed (1 Kings 2:8-9). Next, the king meets a distraught Mephibosheth who claims that Ziba lied. Unable to decide who is telling the truth, David divides Saul's lands between Ziba and Mephibosheth.

The Hebrew word for "adversary" (19:22) is *satan*. It refers to someone who opposes another person or God. The word does not refer to a rival of God.

The magnanimous Barzillai accompanies David to the Jordan, but chooses to remain with his family. He sends Kimham (possibly his son) instead.

The chapter closes with a summary of the feud between Israel and Judah. Ancient tribal loyalties could never be fully offset by kingship. The reunion is only temporary.

2 Samuel 20—Joab Regains His Position

Following the bitter words between Judah and Israel (19:41-43) Sheba, the son of Bicri, rebels and leads a minor revolt against David. Fearful that Shimei's words might lead to something more serious, David returns to Jerusalem and promptly dispatches Amasa. A brief delay on his new commander's part leads David to ask Abishai to begin the mission. Hot in pursuit of Sheba, the mighty men of David and the foreign mercenaries chance to meet Amasa. Joab once again shows his utter ruthlessness and kills Amasa.

The troops move on and encircle the rebellious Sheba in Abel Beth Maacah. Wholesale destruction of the city is averted when a wise woman proposes that only Sheba be killed. His head is thrown over the wall, then the rebellion ends. The chapter closes with a list of officials in David's new government.

Sheba is a Benjamite, and that a Benjamite incites rebellion is not surprising. Both Saul and Shimei are Benjamites. Usually, the blowing of the horn is a call to war; here it signals the withdrawal of the Israelite contingent from David's procession to Jerusalem. "Every man to his tent" usually ends a war, but here it functions as a call for revolt. David ignores this defection until he has reached Jerusalem and settled affairs there.

David's earlier appointment of Amasa as the new commander of the general army (19:13) now proves to be ill-advised. Amasa is inadequate as a leader. The reasons for his delay beyond the appointed time are also unclear. Whether he is busy preparing his own troops or laying ground for another revolt, we do not know. But David does not wish to risk the latter or tolerate Sheba's divisiveness any longer. He sends Abishai to punish Sheba. Joab wastes no time in regaining control over David's army. The unfortunate Amasa falls victim to Joab's blood-soaked dagger.

Meanwhile Sheba has fled to a prominent city in the northern part of Israel, named *Abel Beth Maacah.* The rampart erected against the city wall confirms the seriousness of the battle. A wise woman once again intervenes. (See 14:4-20.) Her wisdom keeps the city from being destroyed and ends Sheba's rebellion. She quickly gains the support of the citizens and Sheba is killed. His head is thrown out to Joab.

This list of government officials contains some points of difference with the earlier list in 8:16-18. The order of the officers is different. The secretary is named Sheva instead of Seraiah, although they may be the same person. Ira is listed as a priest instead of David's sons. Also, a new office now exists, that of director of forced labor.

With two rebellions successfully put down. David now can turn his attention to determining his successor. Peace prevails and the land is united, at least for the moment.

DIMENSION THREE:
WHAT DOES THE BIBLE MEAN TO ME?

2 Samuel 17:1-23—Confidence in God

When the counsel of Ahithophel is disregarded by Absalom, he makes a fatal blunder. However, more study indicates that this was no accident. The discrediting of Ahithophel's advice is an answer to David's prayer in 2 Samuel 15:31. History is shaped by the Lord's indirect involvement in human affairs. And here, the involvement comes as an answer to a prayer.

Most persons believe that God answers prayer. Scripture teaches us that this is true, and our experience confirms it. Our prayers may not always be answered affirmatively. In fact, it may seem that in our experiences, God answers some of our prayers, but not others. Unfortunately, we are not furnished explanations for God's decisions on our requests. We simply may not understand why God honors this or that request.

But what we may affirm in faith is that God does respond to our prayers. Can you make this affirmation? How has God responded to your prayers?

2 Samuel 18:24-33—Paternal Love

David had every conceivable reason to despise Absalom, yet his love remained undaunted. What are some of Absalom's treacherous acts against other persons, including his father?

When David learns of the death of his rebellious son, he cries out in anguish, "O my son Absalom! . . . If only I had died instead of you." These words have become almost proverbial as expressions of a father's grief for his son. No doubt part of the king's grief could be explained as guilt from his own misdeeds. But even so, David's sentiment is genuine and pronounced. His love for his son does not depend on Absalom's performance.

In a like manner, God's love for us does not depend on our performance. Christ came into the world to save sinners, and that means us! Even with Christ active in our lives, we are human beings and therefore prone to sin. We make mistakes, consciously and unconsciously. Yet through it all, we have the assurance that God loves us despite our sinfulness, and that there is true forgiveness to those who turn to God. What relationship does John 3:16 have to this theme?

The Spirit of the LORD
spoke through me (23:2).

—— 13 ——

The Last Words of David

2 Samuel 21–24

DIMENSION ONE:
WHAT DOES THE BIBLE SAY?

Answer these questions by reading 2 Samuel 21

1. Why is there a famine for three years during the reign of King David? (21:1)

2. How does David resolve the claim of the Gibeonites? (21:8-9)

3. Who mourns the death of her kinsmen and protects their bodies? (21:10)

4. What response does her mourning evoke from King David? (21:14)

5. With whom does Israel go to war? (21:15)

6. Why is David restrained from participating in further battles? (21:16-17)

7. How are the four Philistine soldiers killed by David and his servants described? (21:22)

Answer these questions by reading 2 Samuel 22

8. How does David describe God in the first part of his hymn? (22:2-4)

9. What is about to happen to David before the Lord intercedes? (22:5-6)

10. Why is David on the verge of death? (22:18-19)

11. Why does David feel the Lord has rewarded him (22:24-25)

12. How does the Lord treat the crooked and the haughty? (22:27-28)

13. Who is this God who helps David? (22:32)

14. How does God appear to the just ruler? (23:4)

15. What has God done for David's house? (23:5)

16. What are the names of David's mighty men? (23:8-12)

17. Who is the leader of the thirty mighty men? (23:18-19)

18. Who is the commander of the bodyguards? (23:22-23)

19. How does the Lord ask David to punish Israel for her sins? (24:1)

20. How does the Lord punish David for his sin in taking the census? (24:15)

21. What does David do to appease the anger of the Lord? (24:24-25)

DIMENSION TWO:
WHAT DOES THE BIBLE MEAN?

2 Samuel 21:1-14—David Ends the Famine

The term *Amorites* refers to the Canaanites, the Semitic tribes occupying the land before Israel entered. The famine was a particularly severe natural calamity in the ancient world, since it could wipe out crops and livestock and thereby jeopardize the existence of the community itself.

Saul's alleged slaughter of the Gibeonites is not reported elsewhere in the Old Testament. Perhaps the reference is to his massacre at Nob (1 Samuel 22). Saul may have included the Gibeonites in his reprisals against the priests who aided David.

The Gibeonites insist that money will not avenge Saul's sin. They demand human expiation. The shedding of blood is to be atoned by the shedding of more blood. David is unable to locate a sufficient number of Saul's real sons, so he must settle for five grandsons.

Rizpah is identified as the mother of Saul's two sons. She appears earlier in connection with Abner and Ish-Bosheth. (See 2 Samuel 3:7.) The corpses lie protected by Rizpah a considerable period of time until rains come and the bloodguilt is satisfied before the Lord. Rizpah's devotion to the bodies prompts David to exhume the bodies of Saul and Jonathan and give the family a proper burial.

2 Samuel 21:15-22—War With the Philistines

This section contains four episodes that are held in common by the theme that Israel's adversaries were giants (usually called *descendants of Rapha*). The stories are highly stylized in nature and may have originated from contemporary documents such as war annals.

The phrase "he became exhausted" may mean that David is growing older, or it may refer to battle fatigue. The expression "lamp of Israel" refers to the king as a source of illumination (guidance) for the people of God. This close intertwining of king and people reflects a prevalent notion in Israel that divine leadership is usually mediated through the king.

2 Samuel 22—A Royal Hymn of Thanksgiving

At the close of David's illustrious career, a hymn stands in summary and tribute. This song of thanksgiving offers a lyrical testimony to David's career and to the intimate and essential role of the Lord. David's life has been nurtured and guided by God, as this song celebrates. The song is not only theologically important, but it is also significant for aesthetics and symmetry.

The introduction in verses 1-6 lavishes words of praise on the Lord. Vivid and evocative terms celebrate the mighty powers of God. The language recalls David's own personal experiences of salvation at the hand of the Lord.

The second section (verses 8-16) describes a theophany, or manifestation of God. Other theophanies in the Old Testament take the form of earthquakes, with smoke, fire, thunder, and a shaking of the earth. (See Isaiah 6; Exodus 3; Job 38.) God is closely linked with events of nature.

The third section recounts the Lord's deliverance (verses 17-46). Important in this section is the emphasis on God's just rewards to the righteous. Here, as elsewhere in the Old Testament, a person's conduct is met by an appropriate response from the Lord. The extravagant metaphors and images in this section bear witness to a deep and abiding faith in God's justice. Repetition and overstatement reinforce the conviction of the Lord's presence in the affairs of persons.

The conclusion (verses 47-51) reaffirms the earlier confessions of faith in the justice of God. The hymn also shows how God's grace is present in the life of King David, and expresses confidence in God's continued blessings to the people through the Davidic dynasty.

2 Samuel 23:1-7—A Poem of David

Following the royal psalm of thanksgiving, a poem of David records some final thoughts. We are reminded of the final words of the patriarch Jacob (Genesis 49) and those of Moses (Deuteronomy 33).

The word *oracle* in verse 1 clearly places David in the tradition of the prophets. He has a position of favor with God. The gift of God's Spirit empowers him to do God's will. This introduction clearly ranks David among the great and inspired leaders of God's people.

The blessing of Davidic leadership, nurtured by the Spirit of God, brings justice, prosperity, and peace to the land. The three similes in verse 4 illustrate the benefits of David's rule and invoke the powers of nature to touch the depths of human spirit.

In contrast with the rule of David, the lamentable fate of the godless holds nothing but disaster. They are victims of the might of God's servants.

2 Samuel 23:8-39—David's Mighty Men

David's army consists of several internal divisions. *The troops* refers to the general army, comprised of men from all the tribes. The *mighty men* are a group of thirty highly trained, veteran troops. The royal bodyguard included mercenaries like the Kerethites and the Pelethites. *The three* were chosen for their bravery during holy war.

David's refusal to drink the water brought to him by members of the thirty (verse 16) is truly the mark of a noble leader. How could he indulge himself at the risk of valuable lives? No wonder his troops remain loyal to him in times of crisis.

Joab is not included among the list of the thirty. Probably, he was universally known as a member. The fact that thirty-seven names appear indicates that the group was replenished as necessary. Periodic additions also explain the difference between this list and the one in 1 Chronicles 11.

2 Samuel 24—
A Census, a Plague, and the Construction of an Altar

The intent of this episode in the final days of King David is to establish the site of the future Temple. The threshing floor of Araunah became the place upon which Solomon built the famous Temple in Jerusalem.

We are not given the reason for the Lord's anger at David. God instructs David to take a census, and then later punishes him (2 Samuel 24:15). Perhaps the census was perceived as an infringement on some divine prerogative.

Why David feels guilty is also unclear. Perhaps the reason was common knowledge at that time, so the biblical writer felt no need to state the obvious. The angel of destruction is a popular image in the Old Testament (2 Kings 19:35). Only at the last moment does David's prayer avert the angel's deadly hand.

David sets up the altar on the threshing floor of Araunah. Tradition places this site in Jerusalem. God's message to the angel ends the book on an upswing. David's favored relationship with God is in good standing, peace is in the land, and matters are in hand. But the question of succession is still unresolved. This urgent issue must await a future date.

DIMENSION THREE:
WHAT DOES THE BIBLE MEAN TO ME?

2 Samuel 21:1-6; 24:1-17—God and Nature

The two disasters that occur in these chapters, famine and pestilence, both result from God's anger. What steps are taken to assuage the wrath of the Lord?

With our scientific understanding of the operations of the natural order, we have difficulty attributing such catastrophes as droughts to an angry God. For most of these events, we have scientific explanations that do not carry us outside the natural laws of the universe. For instance, we know that diseases are caused by germs, not by demons. Yet many stories in both the

Old and New Testaments describe illnesses as caused by evil spirits.

The biblical perspective on events is a theological perspective. The evaluation of a biblical event is drawn in terms of its meaning rather than its scientific character. How can the Bible's theological perspective on events speak to us today?

2 Samuel 21:15-22—Politics and Faith

Among Israel's many kings, David stands out as a model ruler. He embodies the dual qualities of religious faith and political leadership. Such a combination of qualities was rare then, and it is rare today.

Prepare a list of David's achievements as a military and political leader. Then, prepare a second list consisting of David's acts of faith. The integration of these qualities in a single person forms the prototype of the Jewish Messiah. Which of these qualities does Jesus display?

Would such a combination of political leadership and strong faith be well received today? Why or why not?

THE UNITED MONARCHY
Samuel, Saul, David

■ Philistine Cities

SCALE OF MILES
0   5   10   15   20   25   30

Sidon

MT. HERMON

● Damascus

Dan (Laish)

DAN

Tyre

ASHER

Kadesh

Geshur?

BASHAN

Hazor

ZEBULUN

NAPHTALI

Sea of Chinnereth

Golan

MT. CARMEL

MT. TABOR

The Great Sea

ISSACHAR

Megiddo ●

MT. GILBOA

MANASSEH

● Ramoth-gilead

MANASSEH

HILL COUNTRY OF ISRAEL

Shechem ●

River Jordan

THE ARABAH

GILEAD

MT. GERIZIM

EPHRAIM

GAD

AMMON

● Aphek

● Ebenezer

Shiloh ●

DAN

Bethel ●

● Ai Gilgal

Shittim

Keriath Jearim

Geba ● ● Jericho

● Bezer

Mizpah

MT. PISGAH

Ekron ■ Micmash ● Gibeah

Ashdod ■

Beth Shemesh ●

BENJAMIN

Ashkelon ■

■ Gath?

● Jerusalem

Bethlehem ●

Gaza ●

HILL COUNTRY OF JUDAH

Sea of the Arabah (Salt Sea)

REUBEN

PHILISTINES

Lachish ●

Hebron ●

● Aroer

River Arnon

Ziklag? ●

En-gedi ●

J U D A H

● Debir

MOAB

● Beersheba

SIMEON

The Negeb

EDOM